"*Engaging with Jayshree's thought leadership is a treat – she brings a wealth of experience and expertise, channeling the wisdom of personal growth to see around the sharp corners of today's changing landscapes. The Heart of Science series is an opportunity for those who wish to encounter a perspective with substance during times of uncertainty or for those simply seeking a dose of inspiration.*"

— **Rita McGrath,** Best-selling Author and Professor, Columbia Business School

"*Innovation knows no bounds, which is what we learn from those that dare to blaze new trails into the unknown. From that perspective, among others, Dr. Seth is a role model and Engineering Fine Print offers the space to consider how we move forward individually and collectively to encounter grand challenges and new paradigms.*"

– **Gitanjali Rao,** Scientist, Author, and *TIME* 2020 Kid of the Year

"*Just as the intersections among rapidly evolving disciplines have driven scientific and technological progress, The Heart of Science series explores cross-currents between that progress and societal needs and belief systems. Through autobiographical reflections of her career in science and science communication, Dr. Jayshree Seth urges "compassionate reason" as a tool to navigate the sometimes conflicting perspectives of science and societal beliefs, encouraging ongoing dialogue. An insightful and inspiring analysis.*"

— **Susan Hockfield, Ph.D.,** MIT President Emerita and Author of
The Age of Living Machines: How Biology Will Build the Next Technology Revolution

"*Engineering Fine Print is a must read for those who are grappling with the rapidly shifting landscapes in business, product development, and life. Teasing apart the impacts of major disruptive events, Dr. Seth humanizes the experience of engineering and science within the context of growth and leadership. She brings together the complexities we've collectively faced from a vantage not often expressed with her uniquely creative acrostic style and sophisticated sense of sass.*"

— **Brian Solis,** Best-selling Author of *Lifescale* and *X:*
The Experience Where Business Meets Design

"*Heartfelt, passionate, and deeply personal, Engineering Fine Print is a collection of essays that unpacks the individual, cultural, and organizational barriers so many Asian heritage professionals encounter throughout their careers. Weaving in accounts from her own career and life journey, Jayshree explores the critical role that science plays in bringing hope to society. She embraces the beauty of dialectical thinking as an aspect of leadership guided by her own Asian heritage.*"

— **Jane Hyun,** Author of *Breaking the Bamboo Ceiling: Career Strategies for Asians*
and Co-Author of *Flex*

THE HEART OF SCIENCE

Engineering Fine Print

Jayshree Seth, Ph.D.

First paperback edition, March 2022

ISBN 978-0-578-36995-2 (paperback)
ISBN 978-0-578-36996-9 (eBook)
Library of Congress Control Number: 2020920790

Edited by Eli Trybula
Book design by David James Group, Lombard, IL
Advised by Sharon Jenkins and MC Writing Services, Houston, TX
Cover illustration by Cheryl Peaslee, Warrenville, IL

Published by the Society of Women Engineers
1300 East Randolph Street, Suite 3500, Chicago, IL
+1 (312) 596-5223 | www.swe.org

CONTENTS

I'll Be FINE:
Put It in Print

And...I want to write a book.

Whether it was in essays, interviews, or my dreams, as long as I can remember I would talk about writing. While growing up, I never thought of myself as the *typical science and engineering type*. You know, the kind that like to play with tools, tinker with stuff, or tear apart their toys. I was always more interested in the human context – *I liked humanities-related subjects simply because I could relate to them more.* I enjoyed social studies, the fascinating history of people, the human geography, and the political and civic relationships at play. And I loved creative writing – I wrote articles, speeches, poems, and parodies.

I admired doctors and their ability to make people feel better. I specifically recall a book on the human body that our parents had bought for us when we were very young, and I was fascinated by what was inside all of us. *Maybe I could be a doctor,* I remember thinking. The frog dissection in school made me squeamish, and my brother took it upon himself to inform me that I probably wouldn't enjoy cutting open cadavers. Maybe I wasn't cut out for it, but what was still alive and well was my desire to help improve lives and make the world a better place. At the time, I didn't necessarily associate engineering with such goals.

Regardless, somewhere between Greek tales and Indian mythology, between the fables of talent and the goddess of learning, I pledged that I would put any innate skills I would be blessed with to good use. I remember that exact moment, gazing up as a young girl at the abode of the deity with multifaceted talents, near Laxman Jhula, on the banks of the River Ganges.

BLOOD PRESSURE

Growing up in a home with an engineer dad, on the campus of one of India's top engineering schools, surrounded by STEM professionals, I had strong parental guidance that directed me to engineering, despite what I perceived as my lack of affinity for the field. There was peer pressure too, as most of my friends were striving to get into the hometown engineering school as well, with strong push from their parents. I did, however, have the willingness to follow the path laid out before me and give it my all. I have always liked working hard and feel intrinsically motivated to do the best I can. So, after engineering college came graduate school, and then marriage, and kids, and work, and life.

As a milestone birthday approached, with no book in sight, I had a sense of uneasiness. I know this feeling; it throws me off-kilter. I am then consumed with doing something about it, about making it happen. With immense help from my amazing husband, I compiled some of the nursery rhymes I had transliterated into Hindi for my kids. Accompanying illustrations were made by my son with creative input from all, including my then kindergartner daughter. Right before the stroke of midnight, we uploaded the book into a self-publishing site, and there – it was my birthday, and I had a book to my name.[1] *Namaste!* Thanks to my friends and family who bought copies. We matched the funds from the proceeds and donated the small amount at the deity's altar. And life went on.

PULSE CHECK

Then came 2020 – a year of reckoning in many ways for virtually all of us. A year where many experienced some cycle of shock, numbness, denial, anger, fear, panic, guilt, gratitude, and hope...and then the intense desire to help and be productive... with purpose. I questioned my own identity and reflected upon my intersectionality. I wrote essays about the multitude of crises, the global pandemic and its fallout, and the raw and real exposure of systemic racism on the world's stage. I wrote about how 2020 threw many of us off-kilter.

In my case it often goes something like this:

Crisis → Cry Sis → Cry Cease → Seize → Carpe Diem

I know that feeling. I needed to do something about it. *Acta, non verba.* When you sense dissonance within your communal mindset, you tend to reevaluate what you are doing and how you could, or should, change it. Essentially, you are missing something; *something just doesn't feel right about what you are doing.* It's referred to as *communal goal incongruity* in psychology.[2] A collective sense of communal goal incongruity, and the visceral compulsion to do something about it, led to many positive outcomes in 2020.

My husband and I decided to start an endowed scholarship at the University of Minnesota College of Science and Engineering, in part with 3M's matching gift program. The scholarship supports Black students – it is named the *Sankofa* Scholarship. The word resonated during my trip to Ghana for a 3M-sponsored community service project in early 2020, days before the lockdown. *Sankofa* in the *Akan Twi* language essentially signifies that the past can illuminate the present. My husband and I hope that the horrific event in Minnesota in 2020, George Floyd's murder, will inspire many to commit to change and use one's own pockets of privilege to ensure a just and equitable future for all. Racial disparities resulting

---

[1] Seth, J., 2008. *Namaste! Namaste!...and other Hindi songs based on popular nursery rhymes*, self-published, Blurb.
[2] Diekman, A.B. & Steinberg, M., 2013. Navigating Social Roles in Pursuit of Important Goals: A Communal Goal Congruity Account of STEM Pursuits. *Social and Personality Psychology Compass*.

from systemic racism impact many aspects of Black lives, including the lack of representation in STEM. We felt that this inequity must be addressed, since STEM professionals and academics have a huge influence in shaping our future world – we hope the Sankofa Scholars go on to become role models for others.

HEARTBEAT

The intense desire to do something is also what prompted me to make a call to Karen Horting, CEO of Society of Women Engineers (SWE), in the summer of 2020. *Could we publish a book on some of the lessons learned in my STEM career journey thus far and have all proceeds go toward a scholarship for underrepresented minorities in STEM?* There was no hesitation from Karen's side – none. It was a done deal. There was complete congruity in our communal goals. It took late nights and weekends to finish up the book with help and guidance from the quickly assembled team, and we launched at #WE20: *The Heart of Science: Engineering Footprints, Fingerprints, & Imprints.*

Fast forward to 2021, almost exactly one year later, when I had the amazing opportunity to meet the first recipient of the SWE scholarship funded from the proceeds of the sales of my book. It was one emotional day. My heart was filled with gratitude toward one and all who bought the book, supported the cause, and gave this gift of education. My heart beat fast, and my eyes scanned the room in anticipation. I tried to hold back my tears, crier that I am, as I embraced this young scholar pursuing mechanical engineering at Georgia Tech. This was the same school my firstborn had attended, the same school where I was invited to give a prestigious named lecture. And it just so happened that the event was in-person. I got to meet her. *It's a sign. What are the odds?* I thought. My heart, it said, the universe is sending a message. One book. One scholarship. One student. It all starts with the power of one. *I need to write Book 2!*

I decided to do a LinkedIn poll, and 86% of the respondents agreed that there should be a Book 2 – 7% said "no" and the remaining 7% voted for "maybe."

Maybe I needed to call Karen Horting, once again.

VITAL SCIENCE

The first book in the *Heart of Science series, Engineering Footprints, Fingerprints, & Imprints,* is a collection of essays on several big picture topics from my experiences as an engineer, a parent, a science advocate, and a thought leader. I cover themes such as the need for STEM advocacy, convergence of STEM and humanities, leading from our own rung of the ladder, and developing a growth context. What is at the heart of my second book, *Engineering Fine Print,* is an attempt to go deeper on the topic of **transitions** to thrive and survive amidst change, *reflections* to provide perspective, and insights into **actions** we can take.

And again, as in my first book, I share what has enhanced my own learning and provided me rich context to develop easy, memorable ways to incorporate insights into my own thinking – and my own being. I love the beauty of language, the power of words, and the magic of letters. Pithy phrases pique my interest, metaphors move me, and I am enthusiastic about experimenting with acrostics. Taking the next step from points to ponder that were throughout the first book, I explore the *fine print* with each article throughout this book.

The last two years have made me realize that regardless of what educational path we follow and what career we end up in – *real growth, true leadership, and self-actualization* comes from getting in touch with our *feelings* and dissecting them, understanding our *sense of identity* and its evolution, tapping into our *needs* at a very innate human level, and integrating these new learnings with our *experiences*, to work through tough transitions, deep reflections, and meaningful actions. At the end of the day, it is about what is inside all of us – it just takes time to notice, read, and realize the **FINE** print:

Feelings

Identities

Needs

Experiences

For many of us, the pandemic has really put the lens on this fine print. A time when virtually all of humanity faced the same threat, confronted the same fears, and awaited the same gift of science in the vaccine – *a lot was brought to the forefront.* There was an unprecedented feeling of stark vulnerability and sense of collective grief that many hadn't felt before. It reasserted the need for social connection and the importance of family and friends. It also highlighted the need for self-care and developing resilience. The importance of health and healthy lifestyles was also brought into prominence with many feeling the need to connect with nature again and rejuvenate in a meaningful way. Our experiences in our jobs magnified the inequalities in society and the privileges we may enjoy. That in turn helped us to develop a sense of empathy and gratitude. Our relationship with science and technology, for many of us, evolved and so did our skills – we pivoted to adjust to change.

A new paradigm has emerged in our relationship with change as we have responded to the change around us. We have transitioned, we have reflected, and we have acted upon the change, organically. We have a new lens on life – *it's a fine one.* It will forever change the way we view change and our own abilities to drive change. And that's something to write home about.

Be good. Work hard. Live well.

SECTION 1

TRANSITION

*Times of transition are a great teacher. The **guru**...teaching us how to accept change, helping us to manage change, and leading us to create change.*

LOGIC Test:
Of Guts and Intuition

Should I? Maybe I shouldn't? Right? I think so?

In the height of the pandemic, thoughts like these played over and over again in our heads. Almost every decision had to be a measured one, weighing pros and cons before moving forward with a sense of unease, regardless of the decision. We learned a lot in the preceding two years and are better equipped for a transition out of the pandemic – even if a sense of uncertainty lingers with COVID-19 variants. By the time 2022 started, many of us were hopeful that we would be done worrying about *all things pandemic.* For many others, it felt like a punch in the gut – a new year that, at first blush, seemed old! But intuitively, we all know that a mere change in the calendar doesn't change things overnight.

What did change many things, virtually overnight in many cases, was the pandemic. It brought into focus that we could all operate from different realities, and that different frameworks of thinking could lead to different conclusions. The major divides on several fronts were magnified as the logic behind our decisions and the fears driving our actions were unmasked. The pandemic has become a test case for how important historical and contemporary contexts are, and the role they play in feeding people's intuitions and shaping their views. Our collective survival and ability to thrive may depend upon our ability to come together, and be willing to learn together from the many lessons it taught. Given what we have all experienced, a new call to action is only logical.

CRITICAL ANSWERS

Balancing knowledge and uncertainty became a very distinct feature of life during the pandemic. The intense deliberation required for making seemingly simple decisions to mundane questions certainly took major adjustment.

Do I really want to go to the store?

Should I avoid it as long as I can?

Is meeting a friend in the park okay?

Should we just do a virtual gathering?

Soon enough, we all got better at reviewing the information at hand, getting a sense of calibration from others, and oftentimes postponing decisions that could wait until more data was available. However, the sheer number of decisions that needed to be made each day added to the mental fatigue, especially decision making in a deliberate fashion about things that in the past were no-brainers.

It was a tough time of transition as it relates to decision making – I can say that decisively. Sometimes it brought out our worst fears – we have all seen the news about hoarding toilet paper, while sometimes, despite the risks, we decided to show up in solidarity at crowded social justice marches. We all developed what has been referred to as our own "pandemic logic."[3]

This logic had not just emotions but a whole lot more wrapped into it. It was also evolving, and often impacted by the latest conversation or text exchange we may have had. Wondering, were others paranoid, were they ill, were they grieving, were they depressed, were they overly optimistic? We weighed the decision of how others' conclusions should impact our own pandemic logic. It laid bare our mental processes of synthesizing and digesting, arguing and rationalizing, negotiating and accepting when in crisis mode. It also honed our critical thinking skills. And, as bigger decisions needed to be made, perhaps in many ways, we became more critical and less thinking as data, information, and personal interpretations flooded our mind-space to fill in the blanks while scientists, policy makers, medical professionals, corporations, and government worked together to determine collective course of action. Some days the most logical and easiest decision was to virtually tune out. It was a matter of survival.

THINKING, CRITICALLY

The pandemic has also been dubbed the *infodemic* because misinformation and disinformation were rampant. Misinformation is information that is simply wrong, while disinformation is often categorized as information crafted or curated with an intent to mislead. At a time when virtually all of us had a sense of being ill-informed – whether the situation unfolded with spread of infection, prediction models, public health measures, and medical therapies – the barrage of fake news and half-truths added to chaos and confusion. It impacted how well the pandemic could be contained, managed, and cured. The spread of incorrect information also impacted lives and livelihood as evidenced by irrational fears, episodes of racial prejudice, and rejection of simple public health guidelines. By all means, the nascent realities of the *infodemic* also wreaked havoc on our evolving logic during the full-blown pandemic.

For many, the lack of reliable information, and resulting lack of clarity,

[1]Baratta, M., "Pandemic 'Logic': What we tell ourselves to survive," *Psychology Today*, October 15, 2021.

heightened a sense of fear and anxiety, severely impacting decision-making systems. And deep misinformation contributed to unlikely scenarios, rife with convoluted logic, that were often shared widely, further impairing decision-making for many. With a vacuum of a consistent narrative, which was difficult to assemble given the ever-changing situation and the millions of voices on the media, pandemic logic relied heavily on gut feel and what made intuitive sense to each individual. As a result, it often made us all arrive at different conclusions, causing a divide. Virtually everyone lacked the knowledge and expertise, and yet everyone had to make the best decision possible with limited data, often unvalidated – interpretations laden with bias. It highlighted the importance of critical thinking skills – vital skills that among other things require a conscious effort to gather all relevant information, minimize error, and overcome bias.

CRITICAL CALLS

Critical thinking is often defined as purposeful, reasonable, and reflective thinking when faced with complex issues and conflicting situations.[4] Exercising critical thinking allows one to make a well-thought-out, logical decision on what to believe or decide to do. It typically involves at least two key aspects. The first aspect, *inquiry*, represents the finding of relevant information, critically examining it, questioning validity of assumptions, and essentially synthesizing the information. The second aspect is *argumentation*, which signifies reasoning that supports an idea, theory, or action – the goal being to support one argument in light of the evidence, weakening the other position.

Scientific thinking, under the umbrella of critical thinking, but not to be confused with it, is the thinking that makes meaning of information in scientific domains using scientific methodology supported by sufficient evidence. Scientific thinking allows us to generate knowledge to understand the world around us, while critical thinking involves examining multiple points of view, comparing them, and making a judgment on which perspective prevails, given the evidence. Critical thinking calls for making a call. Scientific thinking seeks evidence to establish objective reality. Interestingly, during the pandemic, a lot of the opinions that ran counter to established recommendations, or showed hesitancy in following them, were also attributed to self-proclaimed "critical thinking" and sometimes even supported by pseudo-science. Though scientific discovery and associated innovations yielded policies, protocols, and ultimately the vaccines, science does not make decisions at the end of the day. Decisions are made by people, and people have their own logic for making the decisions they do make. For science to provide

⁴Muis, K.R., et al., 2021. Epistemic Emotions and Epistemic Cognition Predict Critical Thinking About Socio-Scientific Issues, *Frontiers in Education*, 6, 121.

the desired outcome, it became clear that there is a critical role for critical thinking, among other things, to actively debunk lies and conspiracy theories within the ever-evolving human context.

CRITICAL JUNCTURE

This time of great change has taught us not just about how we make decisions, but how to make better decisions. In crisis mode, our minds implored us to develop our own decision-making framework by taking external information and trusting our own gut, believing our intuitions to help us cope and allow us to survive – *this at a time when we were stretched, stressed, and spent.* Our logic may have seemed illogical through the lens of others, but now, as we move forward, there is substantial evidence, there are validated data sets, and expert advice exists. So, how do we build better logic that can be viewed through a wider collective lens? It is important to have a view of the mindset and frameworks others operate in, not just our own way of thinking and acting based on our own way of being. It is time to update our logic – we can use scientific thinking to develop a robust framework, given the observations, hypotheses, and data from how things played out during the pandemic. It is a critical juncture that we are at – and there is a need to give grace and bring people together on many fronts. Critical thinking will be required at every step along the way.

Changing of minds is not easy. There was validation of the fact that humans typically don't "do" until they can "think" and "feel."[5] During the pandemic, given the urgency, there was perhaps a rush to move, to do, without ample opportunity to process through, to think and feel. And, given the gravity of this situation, shaming can be a counter-productive tactic. Pushing to convince with facts and data, to prove others wrong with logical arguments, does not work either. Humility is key, and it takes more of a collaborative process with active listening and sharing of one's own reasoning to be convincing. Situations like these warrant careful consideration of conflicting viewpoints and open-mindedness to ideas, options, and opinions. Empathetic listening allows understanding of barriers, beliefs, and biases that drive choices. It can give information regarding reasoning for mistrust, doubts, or skepticism. It also allows deeper insights into the emotions and motivations behind the behaviors, the feeling in the gut that guides logic and feeds intuitions.

CRITICAL SKILLS

Building relationships, partnerships, and friendships are key to building bridges. Changing minds is typically not a simple logical appeal armed with scientific data

---

[5]Deshpandé, R., Mintz, O., & Currim, I.S., "3 tactics to overcome COVID-19 vaccine hesitancy," *World Economic Forum*, June 28, 2021

and evidence because it involves not just cognitive but emotional change. And the stories we store in our brain, not numbers and facts, often guide our logic. Context is key, and storytelling with compelling positive narratives of hope can be powerful means of changing hearts and minds. It is time to come together and learn from each other, from our guts, our intuition, and the importance of our **LOGIC:**

Listening to learn

Outreach with open-mindedness

Grace and gravity

Insight from information

Context in communications

Times of transition are a great opportunity to look back at lessons learned. The pandemic has taught us some important lessons regarding the public perception of science, the importance of science communication, and how the scientific method and critical thinking can interact with human reasoning.

It has also taught us how our logic evolves as humans to ensure our individual survival. Now, it is perhaps time for our logic to evolve so we can collectively thrive – from each new year and beyond.

— FINE PRINT —

On a personal note, I still vividly remember the range of emotions I felt as I watched the news every night in my hotel room while in Ghana during March 2020. A group of us were there for a 3M community service project, and the daytime was packed with fieldwork and meetings. Every night, the sinking feeling of an impending pandemic was getting stronger. Fear was replaced by relief as we reached home and shortly replaced by anxiety as the lockdown went into effect. It was a constant barrage of emotions thereafter – a feeling of feeling feelings that hadn't been felt in a long time in quick succession. We often cycled through all of them in the same day.

The mother in me was worried sick about my adult kids, and the adult in me worried about my aging parents and family thousands of miles away. Meanwhile, the scientist in me searched for information, learned about the virus and the prevalent theories and predictions, fact-checked resources, cross-referenced articles, and started tracking reliable sources and credible voices. As all of us hunkered down under the same roof there were decisions to be made – routines, rules, and repercussions. And all of us had developed a pandemic logic that needed to be discussed, argued, and reconciled. After all, each person's behavior had the potential of impacting everyone else. Not all discussions were calm and not all calm was peaceful, but we managed to get along with compromises made along the way.

Having grown up in a country where we wore our childhood vaccine imprints as badges of honor, I was excited to hear of the news of breakthroughs and successful trials of multiple vaccines. I had seen the impact of devastating diseases on an uncle who had polio as a child and a cousin aunt who had smallpox – India's vaccination campaigns were so successful that both of these diseases were eventually eradicated due to this gift of science. This contextual backdrop was a critical element for my decisions. Being vaccinated also emboldened us to make the decision to go to India to finally see family after two long years. Emotion was certainly a factor in that decision.

The pandemic taught me a lot about myself, my own decision-making process, and coping mechanisms. I threw myself into science advocacy activities that could be done in remote fashion and filled my days with events, while working on my first book every free minute I could find. The need to be purposefully productive was so important for my well-being. Given that, I did not miss the in-person interactions as much as my introvert husband did. He decided to take on sour-dough baking and committed himself to perfecting the art. So many more nuances of our identities were revealed through this experience and some defied logic.

The pandemic has been a unique experience that we all need to take learnings from – *our reactions, reflections, and actions* – as we transition toward the *next normal* to become a better version of ourselves. We certainly should. Yes, I think so.

———

It's a Wrap!
Roll the CREDITS

"Do you see what I see?"

What a year 2020 ended up being! The beginning of a new decade, it gave us a great tagline – one that motivated us with a powerful metaphor for clarity of vision. In *Engineering Footprints, Fingerprints, & Imprints*, I talked about using the 20/20 metaphor for a sharper focus on the future, proposing that the way vision works can inspire us to work our vision with a keen eye for prioritization, focus, and execution as the year began. *Lights, camera, action!*

HINDSIGHT 2020

Now, of course, we have come to realize that a mere quantitative assessment of 20/20 was not enough to ensure vision clarity. In hindsight, we learned that the quality of vision is affected by many elements, putting a magnifying lens on the overall picture of what constitutes vision clarity. 2020 is behind us but I still find the science of vision and eye metaphors very powerful in helping to understand what we saw and drive the change we need to see. In fact, it was almost prescient that I had also mentioned the importance of the qualitative attributes for effective vision: *peripheral sight, eye coordination, perception of depth, ability to focus,* and *color perception,* among others.

In looking back at the events that unfolded, it is clear how the inability to see what was going on at the edges derailed our vision. There had been warnings about an impending virus outbreak and the vulnerabilities of the response mechanisms, but it was difficult to put pandemic preparedness into focus given competing priorities. We were also unable to effectively coordinate what the two eyes see and collaborate to blend it together for an accurate representation. Political agendas and personal viewpoints got embroiled with public health measures, adding to confusion. The collective lack of rapid focus adjustments, and the inability to hold the focus in a sustained manner, contributed to chaos caused by the resulting blurred vision.

As the year and the pandemic progressed, waves of civil unrest started, precipitating a cultural race reckoning, and that too spread around the world. This resulted in the year becoming further compounded with the inability of many to see things for what they truly were, multifaceted in all their depth, dimension, and detail, including the systemic damage and extreme injustices that had occurred over time. This resulted in deep divides based on points of views. Although the vision was warped...be it the pandemic, the social justice challenges, or the political divide...once the year wrapped, we had the option to treat and correct the quantitative *and* qualitative parameters of vision as we set our sights, yet again, on light, camera, and action.

CORNER OF THE EYE

The loss of *peripheral vision* signifies the loss of a normal, wide-angle field of vision, even though the central vision may be at 20/20. This causes tunnel vision, and we can't see things unless they are directly in front of our eyes, giving little chance to react and adjust course to manage obstacles. The COVID-19 pandemic was not entirely unprecedented, but our collective lack of preparedness, given the tunnel vision, was indeed unprecedented.

And now, with the learning from 2020, perhaps organizations, leaders, and individuals will widen the scope of their peripheral vision. 2020 showed us that there are stark consequences to the blurring out of warnings that are clear and present at the periphery. This would be relevant not just to future pandemics but virtually all issues that played out in a community highly connected at local, national, global, and social levels.

EYE TO EYE

Each of our eyes sees a slightly different image, but the *eye coordination* managed by the brain blends these two images into a singular three-dimensional view. When dealing with muscle weakness in one eye, the brain eventually learns to disregard the image sent by one of the eyes to avoid double vision, resulting in a "lazy eye," the information from which is not collated by the brain. This, if left uncorrected, can impair the visual system permanently.

We have seen the impact of such one-sided, compromised vision across many spheres. At times, it seemed as though our collective consciousness rejected the input of one side altogether. That limited vision caused division in 2020, like never before, along political, economic, social, digital, and demographic lines. This divide played out not just in the U.S. but many other countries around the world. It behooves us to open our eyes to the chasms. 2020 demonstrated that we have to overcome the *laziness*, bridge the chasms, and heal the divides. And healing the divide requires us to civilly engage with curiosity and mutual respect, acknowledge each other's experiences, feelings, and beliefs, and strive to see common ground.

UP TO THE EYEBALLS

With the loss of eye coordination also comes the loss of *depth perception*, the visual ability to estimate the distance between things and their distance from us, as well as the loss of being able to perceive the world in its three dimensions. When you can't see things for what they truly are, it is hard to generate trust, especially in a time of turmoil. A one-dimensional view of multiple, multifaceted, and interrelated challenges in the same year lent itself to mistrust and distrust.

The widespread trust deficit resulted in rampant misinformation, medical myths, and conspiracy theories. In order to successfully transition out of this paradigm we will need nuanced solutions to these complex problems that build, rebuild, and bolster trust at all levels.

MORE THAN MEETS THE EYE

Critical to our vision is also *visual contrast sensitivity*, the ability to distinguish between an object and the background behind it. Low ability to detect contrast results in low spatial awareness, face recognition, and an overall loss of definition. In many scenarios, such as dim lighting, sensitivity becomes even more important than acuity and the visual field.

We encountered such *dimly lit* times in 2020 across so many facets of our lives that understanding the background and the impact of change has been critical. Among them are the protocols and policies many of us experienced as we transitioned to work-from-home and distance-learning modes. Many elements of culture, camaraderie, and connections were difficult to replicate in virtual environments. Shades of gray also abounded as we dealt with the virus, containment measures, and its testing and treatment. It has become vital to understand the background and develop sensitivity as we move forward.

A BLIND EYE

The *color vision* we see is not really the attribute of what we are looking at, but how our brain responds to the varying wavelengths of light. Receptors recognize the different wavelengths, and our neurons pass it along the visual pathway to create the spectrum we see. As a result, it's not black and white as it relates to what specific color we see because each individual may see the exact same color slightly differently. Various conditions can actually create blindness to some, or all, colors. In some cases, there is a weakness in perceiving a certain color, and there is a need for it to be much greater intensity before its presence can be perceived.

KEEP AN EYE OUT

As we age, we encounter *"aging eye," presbyopia*, the gradual loss of our eyes' ability to focus on objects that are nearby. This is often due to reduced flexibility of the muscles and hardening of the lens, making it impossible to see certain things unless we hold them farther out. In order to really focus on things that are up-close, we need corrective measures.

2020 was a year of extreme weather patterns and raging fires. It was hard to unsee the apocalyptic orange in California or the thick smoke plumes in the Tundra or all the way Down Under. On the other hand, as humans took a pause, we also saw the clearing of air, cleaning of water, and animals reclaiming their habitat. Our impact on the environment, and change in climate, was playing out right in front of our eyes, up-close. But we were, in some ways, unable to focus on it. Thanks to 2020, mainstream conversations finally included a realization that climate change warrants immediate attention.

SEEING THE UNSEEN

2020 was also the year where we started to appreciate the things in our lives many of us had taken for granted. The ability to go to work, for kids to go to school, meals at restaurants, and travel to meet family and friends. We lamented the loss of the mundane – seeing colleagues, meeting family, and hugging friends – and, we learned to make the mundane matter.

As we confronted the crises that unfolded, many of us were also able to bring into view things in our *blind spot*. Our own privilege, that each one of us may enjoy, suddenly became very visible and allowed us to develop a keen sense of empathy for those disproportionately impacted. The year also put the focus on self, and supporting one's own self, in many ways. The isolation brought with it regimens for self-care and hacks for self-reliance. The desolation helped build resilience, and self-reflection eventually brought self-actualization for many. It certainly made me reflect and act, and I am thankful that one of the actions was the decision to write my first book.

BIRD'S-EYE VIEW

As far as the pulse of the global public was concerned, the 2020 3M State of Science Index (SOSI) also revealed some eye-opening results. Science skepticism declined for the first time in three years, and trust in science climbed the highest since SOSI began. Healthcare and environmental sustainability remained top issues for science to solve. Other issues were important too, with racial equality/equity in STEM (Science, Technology, Engineering, and Mathematics), emerging as a key concern.

One thing was clear: 92% of the world agreed we should "follow the science" to vanquish this pandemic. As far as societal challenges were concerned, although governments are key, the public expected collaboration across government, non-profits, the private sector, and even individual citizens to drive real change. In fact, the spotlight in 2020 was on individual acts of kindness and innovation that give hope and inspire.

Now that 2020 is a wrap, a year that was called the worst year, a lousy year, and a year that ought to be canceled, we can zoom in on what 2020 showed us as well. It was the year that brought into heightened focus many elements that warrant more thought and our collective action when we roll 2020 **CREDITS:**

    Community and connectivity

    Remote reality

    Environmental emergency

    Deep divides

    Injustice and inequality

    Trust turmoil

    Self-support

Maybe the lesson in the 20/20 metaphor was exactly that – a test, a reminder that we can be lulled into a sense of visual acuity with our ability to see, but we need to examine the other elements to bring into focus what constitutes the real strength of vision. I can see that my own lens has changed – I find that I am more mindful of the above elements and proactive in addressing these topics as we develop strategy at work or formulate thoughts about the world and our collective future.

We got blindsided in 2020, but knowing what we know now, it can help us work toward a *new normal* that is actually a more optimal vision. In my view, the world, as we see it, will be changed forever due to what started in 2020 on many fronts. The crises of 2020 brought a change in how we view things and that change brought opportunity to adjust our vision.

— **FINE** PRINT —

Most people would perhaps like to forget 2020 as if it was cursed by the evil eye or because the crises that unfolded gave us a proverbial black eye– *disease, death, disasters, and divides.* But I feel we need to keep an eye on what the year taught us. Sometimes, we just have to confront reality. 2020 was a jarring reminder of what happens when many things surface that were previously, seemingly, unseen. We will all have moments, in our personal and professional lives, where we will need to confront reality. It may require us to adjust our vision, and it may require us to step up and lead through the crisis. This time of great change in 2020, and the transitions that ensued, can be credited for teaching us a lot.

The pandemic also allowed us all to see that the key to communication in crisis management is messaging that is positive and consistent, allowing people to see social solidarity.[6] Good communication at such times is timely communication – and the kind that acknowledges the challenges with a high level of transparency, shows empathy to those impacted, and offers an assurance of commitment to work through it, together. Research suggests that women are likely to be thrust into leadership roles during a crisis because women may generally rely on styles that build relationships and connections, whereas conventional communication attributed to men tends to be goal oriented and focused on gaining command. It was very interesting to see this play out on the world's stage – the various approaches employed by leaders around the globe and the associated impact.

Formulating a vision that inspires and gives hope is a hallmark of good leadership. But during a crisis, that vision is tested. After the experience we collectively had during 2020, the idea of holding during a crisis resonates for me.[7] *Holding* refers to how someone in authority interprets and communicates what's happening in times of uncertainty. It signifies the ability to think clearly; to orient people's thinking by providing reassurance and helping them stick together. That, in itself, is inspiring because holding can make us feel more comfortable, enabling us to muster courage during the crisis, to confront change, to transition.

Most of us learned to practice holding skills during 2020 – at work with our teams, at home with our families, and even within our very own minds. If I may extend the vision metaphor a bit further, I almost liken

[6]McGuire et al., 2020. Beating the virus: an examination of the crisis communication approach taken by New Zealand Prime Minister Jacinda Ardern during the Covid-19 pandemic, *Human Resource Development International*, 23(4), 361-379.
[7]Petriglieri, G., "The Psychology Behind Effective Crisis Leadership," *Harvard Business Review*, April 22, 2020.

holding to visiting the optometrist – there is a problem with the eyesight, we don't know the exact solution, but we are working to figure it out. As more data and information are uncovered, we will have the tools, tasks, and tactics to get back on track again with a clearer vision. *Hang tight! Hold on!* Till we know more, let's keep doing what is in our control – within our field of vision – and let's wait to hear on things we can't control or can't see clearly, yet. At times like these, priorities change – it is pointless to focus on things we can't shed light on, and, there is no point in action when we can't have the desired focus needed for execution.

Holding allowed us to see our own strengths and abilities to cope, while offering a hopeful, yet realistic, vision of the future. And that's the point – sometimes we just need to inspire with a vision and sometimes we just need to hold the gaze to see through a crisis.

———

State of Science 2021:
HOPE for the Future

Science to the rescue!

If the virus is a villain, science can be called the hero. In 2021, 85% of participants across 17 countries said that science would save us from the COVID-19 pandemic. This built on the 3M State of Science Index (SOSI) results in 2020, which indicated that science became more relevant, more important, and more inherently interesting to the world during the pandemic. Science was having its moment. It was seen as a beacon of hope for the future, and the momentum continues.

Since 2018, we have tracked how the world views and values science through the 3M SOSI – an original, global research survey to explore the image of science. Insights from these studies shape our initiatives and inform our science advocacy efforts around the world. The 2021 results showed that, a year into the pandemic, science brings hope to the world. Interest in science, STEM education, and careers continued to grow. Results also showed that, for people around the world, protecting the planet was a priority that required immediate attention. There was an emphasis on global scientific collaboration for innovation in solving not just current, but any future challenges we may face.

SCIENCE FRACTION

Science skepticism had grown year-on-year before the pandemic. But that trend reversed itself during the pandemic pulse in 2020, and in 2021, the fraction of those who consider themselves science skeptics was at its lowest level since we started tracking. As I mentioned in my first book, knowing that the image of science was improving because of a global health crisis was certainly no cause for jubilation. Nevertheless, the context behind results from the 2021 study suggested that science has had a prominent placement in the story of the pandemic. Science has been the hero, in the forefront, with preventative measures, new treatments, and effective vaccines – all developed using sound, data-driven, scientific methodology by a diverse community of dedicated professionals.

Thanks, in large part, to the progress made in the fight against COVID-19, trust in science remained the highest it's been since we began tracking in 2018. People who agreed that science is very important to their everyday life remained at the highest level as well. And, three out of four respondents said they defend science when someone is questioning it. The pandemic also ignited a renewed interest in STEM careers and education. More than half of the respondents said, during the pandemic, scientists and medical professionals were inspiring a new generation to pursue science-based careers.

Another theme, which was further bolstered since the 2020 results, was a greater focus on environmental sustainability. The pandemic brought a sense of urgency – with the world calling for solutions to mitigate climate change. More than four in five respondents said focusing on sustainability was key to returning to a "pre-pandemic normal," and about three-quarters said that the pandemic made them more environmentally conscious.

SCIENCE FRICTION

Science can serve as a great unifier, with 67% of participants agreeing that science unifies people with differing opinions as opposed to dividing them. But how long will the appreciation for science last? The data points to some early warning signs: 41% believed that appreciation for science may not continue beyond the pandemic. But the solution, in my view, lies within the survey data itself – specifically the increasing awareness from year-to-year regarding the role of science, rising interest in STEM, and the sense of urgency for solving sustainability challenges. Given those trends, I am optimistic that science can maintain its current appreciation beyond the pandemic.

The world overwhelmingly agreed that we need more people pursuing STEM careers. But, access to STEM and inequality remained among top concerns. Seventy-three percent said that underrepresented minority groups often do not have equal access to STEM education. And seven in ten people around the world agreed that there are negative consequences to society if the science community fails to attract more women and girls. The world recognizes diversity can help science achieve more, including greater global collaboration between scientists, more innovative ideas, new and improved approaches to existing research techniques, and more research and innovation to help underserved populations.

It's no surprise that another theme that emerged was of shared responsibility being key to a brighter future. As we continue to face unprecedented global challenges, people unanimously support collaboration between public and private sectors to advance scientific solutions. Survey respondents agreed that countries should work together on pressing issues like pandemics and the environment. And most believe that the private sector has a role to play in solving challenges such as future pandemics, stating that top priorities for companies should be preparing for future pandemics and combating climate change.

SCIENCE FRONTIER

3M SOSI 2021 demonstrated that, as the global community becomes more connected, we have an opportunity – and responsibility – to work together to solve the problems that affect us all. The results can be condensed into a single word – hope. And because of science, more than four out of five people have hope for the future. It is clear that we need to continue to bolster trust in science and deliver on **HOPE**:

> **H**ero-image continuity
>
> **O**pportunity for STEM equity
>
> **P**ath to sustainability
>
> **E**xpectation of shared responsibility

As the world transitions in the process of recovery, let us not forget that it was science that paved the way in the fight against the pandemic, and has a crucial role to play in solving sustainability challenges. Seventy-nine percent of respondents said that science will make it possible to return to a pre-pandemic normal. Let that be a new frontier, and an improved normal, since we agree almost unanimously that it's important to increase diversity and inclusion in STEM. We agree that we need to do more to encourage and keep girls and women engaged in STEM education, and we recognize that they are discouraged from pursuing STEM education, more than boys. Together, we can create a more inclusive, innovative, and collaborative scientific community to solve these challenges and keep the banner of science flying high.

As we take action, the momentum continues. We at 3M invested $41M in STEM education support in 2019, that became critically relevant as schools transitioned to remote learning.[8] When the murder of George Floyd created a unifying moment for equity and justice across the world, we committed $50M over five years to a social justice fund designed to reduce employment gaps among underrepresented and diverse populations.[9] This built on work started in 2018 by the CEO Inclusion Council to increase representation globally. And in 2021, as part of our overall commitment to creating greater equity in our communities, business practices, and workplaces, 3M set a new global, education-focused goal. The company committed

---

[8]3M, "Science at Home," https://www.3m.com/3M/en_US/gives-us/education/science-at-home/. Accessed January 24, 2022.
[9]3M, September 14, 2020. *3M to invest 50 million over 5 years to address racial opportunity gaps* [Press release]. https://news.3m.com/3M-to-invest-50-million-over-5-years-to-address-racial-opportunity-gaps

to advance economic equity by creating five million unique STEM and skilled trades learning experiences for underrepresented individuals by the end of 2025.

3M SOSI results inspire me to take action in my role, not just as Chief Science Advocate, but also as a citizen of the world. I stand with science. It gives me hope.

— FINE PRINT —

Hope is a complex human emotion. It is an expectation of a certain future outcome, a sentiment believed to be a defining feature of humanity, one that played an important role in our evolution. Hope has often been defined by three elements: *positive outcome, trust,* and *agency.*[10] As a result of the pandemic, public trust in science increased, and this trust is crucial to that feeling of hope. Science gives people hope, bringing the acknowledgment that science will play a crucial role in solving problems in the present and the future. But does the public feel the agency, the ability to influence outcomes and make their vision a reality?

It is interesting to note that a recent study[11] documented what scientists feel when they hear the word "science" compared to what the public feels. Scientists overwhelmingly felt joy (40%), followed by "hope" (36%), whereas only 6% of the public responded "joy" but 63% overwhelmingly described "hope." Talk about a contrast in perspectives! Scientists enjoy the act of doing science, but the public expects positive outcomes from what scientists are doing. Understanding these differences, based on different identities, is critical for science to deliver on the expectation of hope. 3M SOSI results have given us a keen insight into what people want science to solve.

We need more people in science, more people to be science-minded, and we need more people who can communicate the social benefits of science. At the end of the day, public opinion can end up shaping national policies, and science needs strong public support and strong policies. We need to give the message that the public has agency, and the messages describing the benefits of science need to come from credible sources.

People currently positively associate science with hope, but it doesn't take much to turn the tide and erode public trust, especially amidst polarizing forces. We have to sell the benefits of science lest it lose its

---

[10]Gallagher, M.W. & Lopez, S.J., 2018. *The Oxford Handbook of Hope,* Oxford University Press.
[11]Newman, T., "Science elicits hope in Americans – its positive brand doesn't need to be partisan," *The Conversation,* July 23, 2020.

appeal and we can't sustain the hope. After all, *"we're in a marketplace, not a classroom."* [12] Given the experience of the pandemic, it is a perfect time to step up on science communication because the public feels the sense of optimism. People saw what can happen when all sectors come together and rally around a cause, and that makes me hopeful. A future vision of a thriving, diverse science community brings me joy.

———

[12]Science Counts, 2018. "How Americans View Science in Society: A Scientific Approach to a Difficult Problem," Accessed January 24, 2022.

TOP Scientists:
Double-Click on What Makes Them TICK

"Drum-roll! And...the winner is..."

Nobel Prize season is an exciting time. As the awards are announced, it is interesting to learn about the scientists and their groundbreaking discoveries. From the workings of the outer space to the inner workings of the human body, the award-winning research spans the spectrum. In fact, the jetlag I was feeling during *Nobel Week*, having returned from a trip to India, can be explained by Nobel Prize-winning work awarded in 2017.[13] Three American scientists were recipients that year for their discoveries of the molecular mechanisms controlling the circadian rhythm – the natural, internal process that regulates our sleep-wake cycles. This rhythm is disrupted when we travel across time zones because of the temporary mismatch between the external environment and our internal biological clock, leading to jetlag. The molecular circuitry of the body's clock responds and adjusts to different phases of the day – *that critical relationship with the external environment makes us tick.*

The Nobel announcements usually also coincide with excitement building around 3M Young Scientist Challenge. As the nation's premier science competition for grades 5-8, it continues to inspire and challenge middle school students to think creatively and apply the power of STEM to discovering real-world solutions. America's Top Young Scientists have gone on to give TED Talks, found non-profits, make the Forbes 30 Under 30 list, and become role models who inspire many other young students.

TOP OF MIND

I've previously written about how, over the years, I have had the chance to interact with these young scientists and get to know them and learn about their projects. I find myself in awe of their desire to solve scientific problems and their innovative efforts toward the goal. The problems they pick aren't trivial and the passion they show is nothing short of inspirational: an 11-year-old trying to develop a mobile app capable of detecting lead in water, a 13-year-old trying to develop a sustainable method of public transportation, and a 14-year-old developing music therapy treatment for mental health improvement. Year after year, we see projects of the

---

[13] The Nobel Prize in Physiology or Medicine 2017 awarded to Jeffrey C. Hall, Michael Roshbash, and Michael W. Young.

same ilk and students with the same dedication toward their endeavors. Through the support of 3M scientists as mentors, these students continue their complex projects and make headway toward working prototypes.

In 2021, we had many projects geared toward healthcare and sustainability challenges. These two topics, as we learned in the 3M SOSI results as well, are top of mind for the general public. It is no surprise they featured in the selected entries, which included development of deep neural networks to more accurately diagnose and treat diseases, personalized music therapy treatment for mental health disorders, a solution for controlling harmful algal blooms, and a way to remove microplastics and oil from contaminated water, to name a few. Most of the students, girls and boys, talked about the sense of purpose they feel in solving such challenges.

In fact, the 2020 winner, Anika Chebrolu, was initially working on in silico methods to identify a lead compound that could bind to a protein of the influenza virus. She was inspired to work on it after learning about the deaths – just in the U.S. itself – every year, despite annual vaccinations and anti-influenza drugs. But when the COVID-19 pandemic started, she pivoted to target the SARS-CoV-2 virus instead.

It has been exciting to see the journey of some of the past winners, like Gitanjali Rao, now the 2020 *Time* Kid of the Year, who held such promise even at a very young age. I remember 11-year-old Gitanjali talking about how she felt when she put herself in the position of those grappling with the issue of lead contamination in their water, and how that motivated her to find a solution. Since then, she has gone on to find additional tough problems to solve, and solving them, while inspiring many other students around the world.

TOP OF THE GAME

As I interact with these students, it is very clear that they are talented. This comes across in their description of their projects, their explanation of why they chose them, and the approaches they have taken to tackle each problem. This comes across despite the virtual format that we had to transition to, given the pandemic restrictions. Their intellectual capabilities are on display along with their projects as they give thoughtful answers to a wide range of questions, and acknowledge the questions their research has raised. It is evident that they are curious about the topic at hand, and that their curiosity drove them to find answers.

In fact, many of the projects start with the student having a curiosity about an observation or a challenge that they or someone around them has encountered. They were unafraid to learn, working hard to gather knowledge about the problem they want to solve, information about existing solutions to that problem, and ideas on how to improve upon them. Perhaps these are the hallmark characteristics of those who go on to become top scientists in their fields. To a casual observer it may seem that their innate talent, keen intellect, sense of curiosity, and hunger for knowledge led them here.

TOP IT ALL...

However, deeper discussions, and their stories, further highlight what it really takes to get to this level. Virtually all of them talk about many failures along the way – paths that were pursued that didn't yield the desired results. The tenacity and persistence they showed has been critical in their journey so far and vital to their success to date. They have demonstrated determination and a sense of resilience that held them in good stead during their projects, which serve well to prepare them for life. They continued on, despite running into challenges – and maintained the same strong sense of initiative that got them on this path to take on a tough problem and apply their talent and intellect to find solutions. That sense of initiative is a critical driver of their continued efforts.

Many start their project presentations with what got them wondering and what they were curious about. But soon enough, you realize the creativity that underlies their approaches to solving the problem. They figured out creative ways to connect and collaborate with those in the field. Some of them had made rudimentary prototypes with common household materials prior to their mentoring sessions, while others had elaborate sketches and designs of their ideas. Many of them had taught themselves programming and computing techniques to further their ideas and concepts. And I must mention that, in addition to being creative scientists and innovators, many of these students were also very accomplished in other areas such as music, dance, or sports.

It is also impressive to see young students who are seemingly unencumbered by prior path dependence to solve the problem and seek out creative solutions boldly. That's a great reminder for us adults – as our curiosity often dims and creativity dulls as we gain expertise and experience. These young scientists are a great example of not just accumulating knowledge about a topic but putting it to action with know-how to turn their ideas into reality. The balance between knowledge and know-how they represent, the iterative strategy most of them used, and the adoption of technology along the way is exemplary from a problem-solving standpoint.

If talent, intellect, curiosity, and knowledge got them started along this path, it is really the tenacity, initiative, creativity, and know-how that propelled them along in their diligent efforts. The double-click, so to speak, allows one to get to the bottom of how they got to the top – what really makes them **TICK**:

Talent *and tenacity*

Intellect *and initiative*

Curiosity *and creativity*

Knowledge *and know-how*

So, how do we inspire more students? How do we get an uptick in underrepresented minorities aspiring to pursue science and become professionals in STEM?

ROOM AT THE TOP

The critical role of strong support from parents, teachers, and the scientific community is very evident in the case of these top young scientists. I have previously talked about "the village" it takes for them to become well-informed problem-solvers capable of navigating uncertainty and complexity. These budding scientists exude personal passion, but also understand the contributions of others and the criticality of support, exposure, and access they have had.

However, the odds are often stacked against those that are underrepresented. Many factors such as gender, race, nationality, and socioeconomic status at birth can serve to impact the outcomes with no relationship to talent, or to effort. In fact, 3M SOSI results reveal that among those who were discouraged to pursue science, a big factor was the inequity they felt related to their race, gender, or ethnicity. If the resources, rewards, and recognition always go to those who have been successful in the past, it fortifies the underlying assumption that only those who have been successful are competent. It is well accepted that it's not just the lack of resources, exposure, and access but systemic "benign discouragement and active exclusion" that can hinder participation and deter bright young minds from pursuing science.[14]

To create more room at the **TOP**, we need to equip them with the **Toolbox**, provide access to **Opportunities**, and address systemic **Privilege**.

I am excited about the multi-pronged approaches we are taking at 3M to support this cause through our STEM initiatives and commitments. With the pandemic, the social justice issues, climate change-related challenges, and the intersection thereof, it is clear that a new strategy is needed to accelerate access and help facilitate success of minority students in STEM.

[14] Lee, D.N., "A Dream Deferred: How access to STEM is denied to many students before they get in the door good," *Scientific American*, January 24, 2013. .

Having more people in STEM professions that you can identify with can help students imagine themselves as STEM professionals in the future. At a young age, it is hard to envision oneself in STEM when there is no one like you to look up to. Role models also serve to enhance student perception about STEM careers and can help boost confidence in pursuing STEM subjects. When I was growing up, I did not encounter a single woman engineer, and I do believe that may have impacted my enthusiasm, or lack thereof, for pursuing STEM fields. In my case, the fact that virtually all my friends were also pursuing STEM made it easier to go along. The environment of the college campus that I grew up on certainly made a difference in that the familiarity with STEM professions was extremely high, given most of our fathers were in STEM. I do wonder if seeing a few women faculty members would have generated more excitement and created more aspirations.

We need more diverse role models, and we need adequate representation of underrepresented minorities in STEM. We also need to drum up support for more diversity in rewards and recognition – from the local to the Nobel level. It's a win-win. It can all add up to make a difference. After all, there is a strong role of external factors in what makes us all tick.

— FINE PRINT —

Interacting with young scientists is a very energizing experience. They are creative and committed and show incredible resilience. We as adults forget that our best ideas can perhaps come when we let our minds wander. But years of training to stick with the task at hand makes it difficult to let the mind step away and roam freely. Despite knowing well that we need time and space to form creative associations that lead to innovative ideas, it is simply hard to find time to think. I find that engaging in intentional thinking time, the mindful time in nature, and making time for other meaningful pursuits helps sharpen creativity, rekindle imagination, and build resilience.

Resilience is key. As important as recognition is for representation, I do feel that recognizing success exclusively can result in widespread perception that the best scientists and engineers seldom fail. I am glad the young scientists talked about their failures along the way; the resilience it imparted in them could be clearly seen in the way they talked about coping with challenges and the confidence to keep trying. Failure isn't only the domain of young scientists, but an inevitable part of the process of design, innovation, experimentation, and research. In many ways, science in itself is about trying, failing, and figuring out what caused the failure – iterating to drive to a logical conclusion.

In my work, sometimes it is just as important to know what doesn't work. We share results of failed experiments or experiments that didn't yield desired results, widely. This allows others who are pursuing similar problems or encountering the same issue we are trying to solve for to see what we have tried and why we think we failed. This discussion of failure, in fact, leads to much richer discussions. I have found that people are able to formulate ideas and creative thoughts when a specific problem that we are encountering can be crystallized. We, as scientists, embrace the idea of failure but have to confront the fact that those outside of the community may have a different perspective.

I have had many failures along the way, but along the way I learned to reframe – *it can't be a failure if we learned something.* It can't be a failure if someone else was able to use what we developed and make it a successful product in their division. It can't be a failure because, given what we knew, not trying was not an option. Reframing is a critical skill – professionally and personally. The narrative around what it means to fail is particularly important for girls who link failure to lack of ability, versus boys who can blame it on circumstance.[15] We will all encounter failure, at various levels and of varying scales. I believe if I gave it my all, we tried the best we could have, and knowledge was gained in the process, it simply can't be dubbed a failure. *Sometimes we have to move the needle to move mountains,* as I like to say it.

Winning gets widely recognized. But scientific success is often built on failure. Talking about failure and its inherent role in the scientific process can be a key to encouraging more underrepresented students to STEM. Winning is so much more about trying – the ability to fail well often holds the key to success.

_____

[15] Simmons, R., "Why Failure Hits Girls So Hard," *Time,* August 25, 2015.

A LENS on Transitions:
Academia to Industry

"Welcome to a Q&A queue...your questions cue me to what is top of mind for you."

Every autumn, the interns, STEP students (Science Training Encouragement Program), and tech aides who worked alongside many of us in the labs throughout the summer head back to school. Interacting with students is a highlight of summer at 3M. In 2021, this included the opportunity to connect with a new cohort of participants in the inaugural ASCEND program for undergrads and the second annual RISE symposium for those in graduate school. Over the years, 3M SOSI data has shown that the global public believes exposure and access are among the challenges that underrepresented minority students face in STEM. To create pathways for that exposure and access, 3M continued to act on its commitment to increase engagement with students in science education and STEM careers.

Accelerating Student & Candidate Engagement, Networking & Development (3M ASCEND), is a program primarily intended to provide first-year and sophomore students with the skills needed to successfully navigate the internship recruitment process. It introduces emerging, underrepresented talent to the wide range of rewarding STEM career options through interaction with 3M STEM professionals. The students learn about different careers, receive advice from recent graduates on how to search for internships, and get tips on how to best represent themselves during the recruitment process. The event is open to individuals in the first or second year of pursuing a bachelor's degree in STEM fields.

Raising Influence in Science & Engineering (3M RISE) provides emerging female and/or underrepresented STEM graduate talent exposure to careers in corporate R&D fields. Students present their own academic research and network with a community of emerging and established scientific talent and hear about their journey and industrial research experiences. The key objective of both these programs is to provide exposure and access to a wide range of careers and professionals. I can personally attest to the important role exposure and access have played in my journey.

For my session, I typically ask the organizers to send my bio to the students and solicit questions for our interaction. I want to know what is top of mind for them and make sure I address it adequately during my presentation. I find that this leads to a richer discussion following my presentation. The typical questions I get usually fall in four big buckets:

1. Questions that relate to the decisions and transitions that are imminent for them,

2. Questions about 3M and what it is like working here,

3. Questions about my educational and career journey, and finally,

4. Insightful questions about overall perspective, work, life, and everything else.

SCHOOLED IN DEGREES

In the last few years, I have reflected upon my own graduate school journey often. To answer the questions around the transition from working in an academic lab in a university setting to research in a corporate environment, I basically drew from my own experiences and associated learnings. I highlighted the fact that a lot about the transition and its relative ease can depend upon the specific nature of the research and one's relationship with their advisor and lab-mates in the research setting, as well as the environment and culture of the academic lab and fit with one's mindset, interests, and working style.

When I was in graduate school, there were professors in my department who interacted with their students often and those who seldom met their students. Some of my peers were actively involved in helping their advisors with grant proposals and some were involved in running the labs, while others also interacted with undergrads in their role as teaching assistants. Moreover, the research work in graduate school can range from very basic sciences to quite applied sciences, and to combinations of the two within the same lab. So, given the range of experiences in the graduate school environment, the transition experience to an industrial setting can also vary.

In my case, there was a more applied sense to my doctoral work. Admittedly, instead of going into depth of just one particular aspect, my work revolved around growing topic breadth and exploring possibilities, which worked well for my interests and mindset. I had switched labs from my master's to my Ph.D. project – from theoretical modeling to a hands-on project – where I could build a stronger problem-solving context, work in a more collaborative environment, and encounter consistent interactions with my advisor.

SCHOOL'S OUT

The transition in graduate school set me up well for adjusting to the corporate environment – working in a division lab at 3M as more of a *generalist*. In this role, as an incoming product development engineer, what I particularly liked was the opportunity to be a part of teams, specifically cross-functional teams with people not just from the various lab functions but also quality, manufacturing, marketing, and sales. The RISE participants appreciated hearing that, as they look to enter the workforce, they can choose to work in the same area as their advanced degree – becoming a subject matter expert within the organization. They can also work in an environment where they leverage what has been learned during graduate work – extending it further within the area and to other areas. And, as in my case – I never worked in the area of doctorate research and have just relied on the basic skills learned during graduate school – to *dig deep and solve problems*. A lot depends upon what you are more inclined to do, what you are willing to learn, and what you are open to – including people management and even business leadership.

At the end of the day, the industry setting is shaped by the fact that the work has to lead to tangible business solutions for the customer, through product and process improvements and related innovation. In contrast, obtaining a degree is the end goal in graduate school, and it is largely driven by the student and their understanding with their advisor. Given the primary objectives in an industry setting, there can be a larger number of collaborators and stakeholders, timelines and deadlines, decision matrices and metrics. However, many academic positions these days may also entail similar settings and associated challenges. At the end of the day, transition is largely about understanding the roles and responsibilities and appreciating the interrelationships and interdependencies. For a role like mine, a scientist in product and technology development, the net you cast to get anything done is typically much bigger; the pace of work is bound by time, driven by the deliverables, rigor, and discipline. The work, and the resulting network, is typically more interdisciplinary. With that comes an appreciation for what are often referred to as "soft skills."

The information from my own experiences resonated with the students. I assured them that if they pick industry jobs, they will likely not give transitions a second thought a few months down the road as they onboard and learn how to navigate. Most organizations have formal orientation processes, buddies, mentors, and supervisors that help new graduates transition on their way to the day-to-day life of a scientist in industry. Many of the questions around what my own typical day is like also centered around the comparison with what they do on a daily basis in graduate school setting. To provide deeper insight, I took the opportunity to give some concrete examples of things in the listed areas I might do on a typical day in my role as a senior scientist:

- Find problems to solve. Collaborate to solve problems.
- Develop technology. Commercialize products.
- Invent. Patent. Document.
- Bench-scale planning to factory-scale experiments.
- Plan for data. Generate data. Analyze data. Digest data. Communicate data.
- Interact with customers. Understand trends. Build strategy.
- Lead projects. Direct teams. Chair committees.
- Learn, unlearn, and re-learn...
  - Read, Classes, Seminars, Tradeshows, Conferences...
- Mentor. Teach. Coach. Participate.
- Internal presentations. External communications.
- Meetings. More meetings.
  - One-to-one, Teams, Group, Function, Lab, Business, Corporation...

This peek into the day-in-life gave the students a good appreciation of what a career in industry could entail. Hearing from other 3M speakers from different functions and at various levels gave good exposure to a multitude of careers and roles.

SCHOOL OF THOUGHT

As students consider what to pursue after their graduate work, I hope to shed some light on what life is like in a corporate setting. Call me old school, but regardless of where a student ends up – *working in academia, government labs, as an entrepreneur, or in a corporation* – at the end of the day it is often more about the mindset and where you focus the **LENS**. For those of us who are in industry, we find ourselves constantly learning, and leveraging what we learn, as we apply science to life. These learnings cast a wide net and so does our work, and network, as we find what works for us to advance our skills and develop expertise. The balance of these elements become the focal point for our journey:

Learning *and* leveraging

Engineering of applications *and* applied research

Net, work, *and* network

Skills *and* subject matter expertise

My parting message to students: Don't fret transitions! Gain exposure and as many experiences as you can while working toward your education. Learn about other areas and fields and collaborate with people from different backgrounds and functional expertise – this helps to hone your skills and helps you learn more about yourself as well. As for back to school, the learning never ends – that's the key to ASCEND and RISE.

— FINE PRINT —

Every summer, as I work with interns or talk to student groups, their questions lead to the story of how my career journey at 3M started – it was as an intern! I tell them how a friend, a fellow graduate student at Clarkson University, accepted a position at 3M at the encouragement of his brother. 3M was relatively unknown to us as graduate students on the East Coast at the time. My friend's brother had joined 3M after graduating from the University of Minnesota (UMN) – many UMN students end up at 3M since it is headquartered in Minnesota. Our friend then encouraged other graduate students to apply for summer internships at 3M. These internships are typically for undergraduates, since graduate students leverage summer months to significantly advance work on their research projects under the guidance of their advisors. Two of us from the lab applied and ended up getting accepted.

Fortunately, our advisor saw it as a learning opportunity for his students, even if it would be at the expense of advancing research. During the internship, I interviewed at another company as well as a group at 3M. I accepted the 3M opportunity. I feel I would have never found my way to Minnesota if it wasn't for this chain of events. In looking back, I truly feel like it was destiny. I tell the students: *Your destiny awaits – oftentimes we don't know what we don't know!*

But back then, I too remember feeling a bit lost the first day of my internship –

What if I can't do what they want me to do?

What if I don't know how to do something that they expect me to know?

What if I am not successful with this project per their expectations?

I share these feelings that I had with students – these are typical questions most of us would ask ourselves. And the answer to these questions, for me, was: *Well, I will do the best I can.*

My fears were gradually allayed as I actually started doing the experimental work. The background was explained to me, as were the challenges that had been encountered by others tackling the problem and the starting point to address it – working alongside with them, on a team. And to this day, I have the very same set of questions with every change, and I know I hold the answer – I will do the best I can. Working through many transitions has taught me that.

———

"Change is made of choices, and choices are made of character."

— Amanda Gorman,
Call Us What We Carry

SECTION 2

REFLECTION

*In a distraction-laden world, with activity-driven days and task-oriented lives...reflection can be the **mantra** to refocus our minds on what matters the most.*

Echo Chambers:
The Sound of SILOS

"Who are you? Really..."

Our nuanced identities, and our own consciousness around our identities, create a complex tapestry. And, it blankets us with comfort as we find our *tribes* – like-minded people who share much of our background, our experiences, or our views. As for me, I am a STEM professional. I am a parent. I am an American of Indian origin. These are a few of the key descriptors that are a big part of my identity. To a casual observer in the U.S., perhaps I am seen as a woman of color in a male-centric profession. The voice in my head tells me I am a well-educated, fairly privileged, South Asian immigrant. And, when among Indians, I am further identified by my language, region, religion, etc.

Weaving all that with my strong personality traits, my rich professional journey, and my diverse life experiences creates the fabric of my being – the backdrop for my mindset – and gives color to my world views. I have been fortunate to find kinship – a few tribes with much diversity – but 2020 showed us that we constantly need to stretch and make sure we think outside our bubbles, hear outside our echo chambers, and look for an objective, outside-in perspective. We all need our support systems and the sense of community that provides a *safe zone*. At the same time, we have to be open to connect with others, seek new connections, and realize that we mutually benefit from that connectedness.

Currently, there is a great realization of the systemic and structural inequities that exist in various aspects of our society and the need for equality, and, an awakening to be inclusive, given all aspects of our complex identities, our *intersectionality*. The word lends itself to the ability to knit together a pattern of experiences based on the many vectors of diversity, including the privilege and discrimination that each may entail. It offers a thought-provoking lens, as individuals, groups, and organizations spend considerable time and effort trying and toying with different ideas and initiatives in an attempt to understand how we address the seemingly elusive goal of true equity and inclusion. This attempt is challenging in view of intersectionality in the broader sense, especially given the draw, familiarity, and validation our own silos can often provide. It may sound simple, but it's not easy – simply because, as humans, we often do struggle to easily relate to others who we see or perceive as *different*.

WHACK-A-SILO

A 3M screening of *Picture a Scientist*, a documentary that chronicles the challenges of women scientists, led to much reflection and discussion. Its release during Women's History Month was a stark reminder that, despite the progress that has been made, there is still a lot of room for open discussions and meaningful action to achieve gender parity and STEM equity. The issue of the *leaky pipeline* is unlikely to be resolved if we don't adopt a holistic strategy, conscious of systemic and structural changes for supporting women in STEM – across the spectrum of lived experience. We need all the diversity and creativity we can muster to unlock the secrets to a sustainable future. At home, in school, as well as in society and throughout our general social conditioning, implicit bias issues are keeping talent away, precisely at the time we need all the creative ideas and scientific solutions to solve the global challenges we face.

The film prompts all audiences, regardless of gender, to question and acknowledge their own implicit bias, especially as the stories implore us to drive change. These include behavioral, ideological, and organizational changes that need to be made to address the problems that have deterred women from STEM education, or from STEM careers despite having a STEM education. Moreover, the race and gender intersectionality, as shown in the film, further compounds the issue. Of course, like many complex and intertwined issues there is no easy or one-size-fits-all solution that falls neatly into boxes to be checked. Taking a simplistic view and assigning labels and categories can often lead to a never-ending game of whack-a-mole in dealing with pervasive bias and inner prejudice as we solve one problem and create another. But acknowledgment and acceptance are key as we move forward toward action, devising informed solutions with a heightened sense of urgency, as well as a need for transparency.

TRICKLE-ME-SILO

Lately, many organizations are doing just that – listening, learning, and re-evaluating their diversity and inclusion goals, strategies, and culture. It makes perfect business sense, not just from employee engagement, retention, and recruitment perspective, but it also serves to increase customer loyalty and brand presence. In addition to grassroots efforts and employee affinity groups, executives have been visible and made clear statements about their commitment and action plans, which trickles down through the organizational hierarchy. Although progress on this front is slow, the appointment of women to board and executive positions can further promote the trickle-down effect. The hope is that the concept of equity is not dealt within a *diversity silo* but becomes a guiding principle in everything we do – with clear mandates and accountability.

It was particularly important and energizing to have many of our male colleagues at 3M participate in viewing the film, and in subsequent workshops, to discuss thoughts and feelings after watching the real-life struggles of the three women scientists portrayed. Many men admitted being shocked and surprised; women, much less so. It is critical to foster these interactions and interconnectedness to avoid silo mentality in the framing of the problem, and in arriving at solutions. We also had many men step forward and hail women in their organizations as trailblazers, changemakers, advocates, builders, and mentors through our #YearOfLift campaign, facilitated by the 3M Women's Leadership Forum. I am particularly appreciative of the *Men as Allies* efforts that invite all to engage in this initiative highlighting women leadership.

Just as it is critical for all women to embrace the concept of racial parity, it is important to see men embrace the concept of gender parity – to show up and speak up. Gender equity and parity in the sciences is not a women's issue alone, women scientists are not role models for women alone, and we need all women to be rightfully *pictured* as scientists, not men alone. As the film showed, sometimes men may be simply unaware of the inequalities or the hidden toll they take. We have to work collectively to understand the issues and break down silos. We need frameworks for action that, instead of creating isolated, stagnant entities, rely on connections, sharing, and flow.

G.I. SILO

Organizational strategies and goals go a long way, but individuals have a very strong role to play to accelerate much-needed change by forging connections across silos and taking action to change the culture. These shifts eventually cascade but can start with one person at a time. To win this game, we do need *action figures* – the kind we had in the film. These brave trailblazers, the three women scientists highlighted – all at different stages in their career – were compelled to take action. They felt injustice and the strong desire to change things for themselves and for future generations of women. Whether it was through collecting data and building solidarity with others to drive action against longstanding inequalities, a quest for justice years later to right a wrong, or through questioning the systems that are often designed to keep people out – their heroic actions made it happen.

When we are too accustomed to gravitating to those who look and act like we do, at work or in our lives, we feel satisfied, and we risk becoming complacent. It may be comfortable, but we inadvertently shun people. We can become closed to new experiences and end up deterring change or progress that it can bring. Progress requires listening, learning, and increasing our *cross-silo* awareness by reaching out to people outside our circles and expanding our sphere of influence, helping them improve theirs. As shown in the film, we all have biases. We need to scrutinize our own prejudices and all the assumptions or excess baggage we carry knowingly or unknowingly. Most of us don't even realize how our implicit notions and entrenched beliefs, buried deep within our identity at some sub-conscious level, impact our subliminal thoughts and overt actions – *who we connect with, what we support, and how we judge.* Although this may be unconscious, it profoundly impacts our habits, assumptions, values, and, in essence, how we *show up* in the world. And, as pictured in the film, it impacts the world.

As organizations work toward dismantling systems and building ecosystem-wide solutions, we as individuals can take action to avoid echo chambers and break our own **SILOS** by paying close attention to the many elements in our lives – at home, at work, and in the community. I have had ample opportunity in 2020 to examine, study, and reflect – I am committed to taking small steps and intentional action across these various aspects to make changes.

> Social circles & spheres
>
> Informal & formal connections
>
> Local community & culture
>
> Opportunity creation & context
>
> Societal constructs & classifications

It's a journey. Maybe the question isn't *Who are you?* but *Who do you want to be?* and *What are you going to do about it?* We can all move closer to the goal by implementing changes at an individual level to impact change at organizational level and societal level.

Picture this. Whoever we are, we are, after all, connected – inextricably so.

— FINE PRINT —

These days, I often find myself thinking about how I grew up and the role it played in shaping my world views. Ours was a block of six homes – at any given time we had more than five religions represented. In this block of six, you could hear six different languages on any given day, including English, spoken by the American family of the visiting professor. You could also smell the wafting aroma of regional cuisines from all over India. We had all regions represented since all of us were from different states. There was also a kid with a physical disability, one who was neurodivergent, and two kids who had been adopted. Religion, language, or customs never got in the way. We all spoke Hindi – some broken, if language was needed to communicate, that is. Otherwise, we all played together and spoke that universal language that all kids who play together develop and understand.

The differences enriched our childhood. These were certainly the perks of growing up in faculty housing on a college campus. The reality of what can go on at college campuses hit me when I left my integrated childhood and joined a college myself. I encountered wonderful, open-minded people, but there were also those who harbored resentment against girls in engineering. There were some targeted microaggressions and a general discomfort towards people who weren't part of the majority. It was a bit of an awakening. It was also a great exercise in building social capital – it happened organically as we were all thrown together. The girls bonded, the folks from specific regions of the country had formed associations, and bridges were built with the other factions – one person at a time. I made attempts to learn the language, as well as build relationships to understand people, and what was behind their perceptions. By the end of four years, most of us had learned to accept each other, differences and all.

Coming to the U.S. was another great training ground. Here, among other things, I learned to code-switch, to use words and accents that helped me navigate my new world – and save my Indianness for those with whom I felt at home. I was the only female in the lab I joined, and I often wonder now if my struggles through my master's program were largely due to the fact that I couldn't relate. Were the biases that were prevalent in the environment the reason why I felt like I couldn't survive or thrive? I switched labs. The Indians bonded, the foreign students formed associations, and bridges were built with the narrow slice of American representation on our tiny college campus.

When I moved to Minnesota to work at 3M, I often found it reminiscent of my childhood. We were on the campus – all with different backgrounds and experiences and functional expertise –all cooking something a little different in our labs, empowered to find a common language and work toward playing together. However, as I reflect upon it, I feel we got comfortable in our new identities, in our silos, comfortable in our ability to navigate and accept standardized experiences. We perhaps rationalized diversity with a narrow lens of "professionalism" while the entire context could have benefitted from some reframing.

Movies like *Picture a Scientist,* or what has played out on the world's stage since 2020, reminds me of the things I, myself, have experienced in my life, but have since been buried deep down – instances of bias, micro-aggression, prejudice, and discrimination. We do need to break our silos and find a better balance in our social capital – *our bonds, bridges, and linkages.* My kids have helped me work through my awakening as they navigate their future, and share their experiences from the past that they have never shared before. My role as Chief Science Advocate has also helped me in reframing the context as I gain better understanding of the issues of diversity, equity, and inclusion in STEM fields. I am thankful that we can all have capacity to learn, at any time, at any age. We all may not be heroes, but we can all take action.

———

August Company:
In the Thinking Corner with KPIs

"Oh! Mommy is fangirling again."

Indeed. I didn't have to look up the meaning of yet another word from teenage vernacular. I knew they must be referring to my religious attendance of the "Friday Fireside Chats" hosted by Rita McGrath. It's one of the *rituals* I picked up during the pandemic.

Rita McGrath, a longtime Columbia Business School professor, is a bestselling author, top management thinker, and one of the world's experts on innovation and growth strategies. I, being an innovation practitioner, have read all her books including the most recent one, *Seeing Around Corners: How to Spot Inflection Points in Business Before They Happen*. As someone engaged in identifying problems to solve, it is always enlightening to read about the latest management philosophies, growth strategies, and organizational tactics to help understand and predict emerging needs and trends. Her work and her wisdom resonate, and so does the weekly webinar with insightful exchanges between Rita and her luminary guests. These are top thinkers, leading experts, and thought leaders.

"Aren't you one?"

"I am what?"

"A 'thought leader'? So, are you going to be on it?"

"On what?"

"Her fireside chat.... What else?!"

"Are you kidding me! This is Rita McGrath...and do you even know who her guests are?"

"Well, I don't know...but she should have you."

I shook my head and went back to listening, but couldn't shake off the feeling – *she done raised the bar on me...ugh-gain.* And she didn't stop there!

"Well...what happened to your you-can-do-anything-if-you-put-your-mind-to-it? Yeah, Mommy?"

Tables were turned. I was in a corner. Yes, I have always told my kids, and my mentees...and yes, myself...that anything is possible. *It's impossible!* said the imposter. It had already come out of the dark corner and invaded my mind-space.

TURNING THE CORNER

Fast-forward. I was on Rita's Friday Fireside Chat! It was a dream come true. Truth be told, it was also a good exercise in quieting the imposter and revving up my virtuous cycle to make this milestone possible. I needed to remind myself of the value of information gathered over the years as a STEM innovation practitioner, the keen insights into the culture, processes, and leadership to support innovation and the intuition sharpened through this journey. It validated that we can all have a perspective, and all perspectives matter, especially if they offer unique insights and creative solutions.

I could hear myself vanquishing the imposter as I answered Rita's insightful questions. I explained my perspective on what drives an innovation culture and the role of employee empowerment to bolster and sustain it. I could clearly see the comments resonate about the importance of the human context in science, innovation, and leadership, as well as the integration of humanities in STEM. I shared my approach to innovation and finding problems to solve – what I call my "mosaic building" process, which was also captured by David Epstein in his book *Range*.

I could sense my own excitement as we talked about an intentional approach to innovation amidst this time of change during the pandemic. And as it relates to the pandemic, it was with much confidence I assured the listeners that science is having its moment – it is in the forefront, and we need to sustain that momentum and sense of hope. Sometimes just talking to yourself and hearing yourself talk are a big antidote as that little imposter feeling creeps in. *Knowing your stuff* pays rich dividends too, but oftentimes it takes reflection and rumination, and it takes practice. Oftentimes, quelling the imposter takes a recognition of ego and humility and practicing the fine balance therein.

AROUND THE CORNER

In my role as Chief Science Advocate, I have really taken it to heart to understand the issues at hand, the data and the stats, and to work at the storytelling aspect, often with my own story as a backdrop. This came in handy when I was invited on the "Leveraging Thought Leadership" podcast. In this podcast, hosts Steve Winick and Bill Sherman talk to guests about best practices in what they refer to as the "business of thought leadership." Bill's guests typically dig deep into organizational thought leadership, as they seek out "professionals who create, curate, and deploy thought leadership on their organization's behalf." The history, and how we continue to build our science advocacy platform at 3M, was a key topic of discussion.

The meaning of "thought leader" as a designation, distinction, or label is often debated and perhaps rightfully so. At some level, every leader is, or should be, a thought leader because leaders are expected to develop a perspective or point of view about a trend, issue, or challenge and need to influence others with associated ideas and insights. By most definitions thought leadership is not about selling products and service. In my thinking, it's about empathy, education, and engagement with an issue or trend that many care about, and the ability to raise awareness, foster conversation, and move forward with credibility and authenticity.

I shared my own personal story and coming into the role of Chief Science Advocate – how my own struggles, my journey, and my experiences in raising kids has shaped my approach to advocacy. I couldn't quite relate to STEM fields when I was growing up. It somehow lacked a connection to the human context that always piqued my interest. I saw the same thing with my daughter – the context was so critical for her while the content sufficed for my son. I strongly believe we can achieve more diversity in STEM fields if we start communicating science with a human context and relay how scientists help people and science can improve lives. We need to make science feel more approachable while raising awareness and appreciation of science in our daily lives. With the pandemic-related challenges the world currently faces, and the sustainability challenges that lie ahead of us, science has a prominent role to play. We need to advocate for science. And we need to break down barriers, biases, and boundaries and advocate for diversity in science. The public agrees we need to do more to encourage women and underrepresented minorities in STEM. The pandemic has pushed women around the world into a tight corner given its disproportionate impact in many ways.

OF WALLS AND CORNER

All in all, I feel truly fortunate to have had the opportunity to share my thoughts at some prestigious forums and learn from the esteemed company. I feel blessed to be able to say what needs to be said, to provide perspective and a potential path forward, and to proactively pull people in. The 3M SOSI, and my own experiences as a STEM professional driving innovation within a large organization, have given rich content and context that I can authentically speak to – and that helps in combatting the sense of imposter syndrome. These are relevant topics with far-reaching implications and are currently top of mind for many. It is great to see that our ideas and insights provide a perspective, and the point of view from my own vantage point resonates with many. It inspires me to continue to take initiative with the incredible opportunity I have been given to share my thoughts and lead for impact outside the four walls of my not-so-corner office. I was truly honored to receive the 2021 Gold Stevie for the inaugural Female Thought Leader of the Year award in Business Products category

"How do we know if we are being successful?"

Bill asked this great question that we think about at 3M a lot: How do you measure success? What are the KPIs, the *key performance indicators,* for this thought leadership platform? There are quantitative metrics and qualitative content that we can and do review, from an organizational standpoint. As for me, personally, I am in the long game; even if we can change one mind, influence one life, and alter the trajectory of one journey, I consider it a success.

The pandemic has really made the public reflect and react positively to the role of science. And as I reflect upon what my KPIs should be, and how they should change given the pandemic and the social justice reawakening, I find myself focusing on the context, inspired by the vision, and committed to the outcome. I do have KPIs; it's my own process for which I hold myself accountable. Am I gathering the knowledge around this topic, am I developing a credible point of view that merits attention, and am I taking initiative and sharing my perspective to foster a conversation? Am I out there leading change with thoughts – and following it up with action? I don't cut corners on these metrics – *my* **KPIs**.

Knowledge or knowhow or research – *that you can authentically own*

Point of view that merits attention – *vantage point that makes it insightful*

Initiative to inform, influence, inspire – *and have impact*

Share and socialize – *simply putting yourself out there*

Action and resulting success go a long way in confidently quieting the imposter. My family too was excited that I was able to make it happen.

"But don't expect me to fangirl you!" said my daughter.

No, not yet! But I know it's coming – we might be at an inflection point. I am seeing around the corner.

— FINE PRINT —

I didn't set out to be a thought leader; my thoughts led me here. And as I reflect upon it – maybe my actions and my words. And that is exactly how I landed up on Rita's show. People have asked me whether I had met her and if that led to this interaction. Well, I have *met* Rita, I say, and I tell them the story that I also shared with her.

It was 2002. I had been selected to attend 3M's new Accelerated Leadership Development Program. I was a bit overwhelmed, *li'l* me from the lab, and no one from my division had attended, let alone the technical community. In fact, I didn't even know technical people could be selected for it. We would be split up in teams and work together for 17 (long) days to tackle a challenge relating to one of 3M's businesses. It was definitely anxiety inducing, and I kept wondering why I was there and whether I deserved to be in the first set of rounds for such a prestigious leadership development program. *What do I know to help other businesses? I am just a scientist in the lab.* However, I did truly enjoy the first week, which was classroom style. We had – what I later discovered – top speakers on the topics of strategy, management, innovation, and leadership. These turned out to be subjects that I intuitively found very interesting and intellectually stimulating, but really hadn't explored much as I was busy with my day-to-day lab activities.

After every few lectures there was a break, and we would rush to the bathroom – back in the day it was a two-stall situation, so the lines took a little while to move. I saw this lady in a powder blue suit at the end of the line and I remember thinking that I hadn't seen her in class, but then again, I didn't know many of the people there – they were all business leaders. I apologetically smiled – the kind of smile you give to people when you reach the front of the line and it's going to be a while for them to make it through. We returned to the class, and it turned out she was the instructor! Every word she said resonated. Of course, we didn't have smartphones back then – I later learned that it was *the* Rita McGrath.

In looking back, I also think about the bias – as to why it never occurred to me that she could be the speaker. It's because they had all been men. I have since bought her books and I try to read all her articles. Once the pandemic started, so did Rita's Friday Fireside Chats. I try to block the time and listen to them whenever I can. And when my daughter challenged me, I wasn't going to give the possibility a second thought – I mean, after all, who am I and why should Rita have me on her program? But, I couldn't get it out of my head – I had to figure out a way to make it happen. After all, the pandemic had changed many things, and the world needs fresh ideas and new inspiration. It could be a great opportunity to talk about 3M State of Science Index results, our science advocacy platform, and how it all relates to bolstering innovation.

What ultimately opened the door for me was the fact that David Epstein had interviewed me for his book *Range*. And why did David interview me? When he reached out to 3M with his hypothesis for his book, one of the innovators they directed him to was me. And why did they direct him to me? They said they had referred me because I had thoughts around innovation that I had put in action and in pictures and in words – and word got around. I had apparently exercised *thought leadership* without even knowing it. And one thing led to another as one thing built on another seemingly unrelated thing. And things worked out for me to feature on Rita's show.

Sometimes we don't give ourselves the credit we deserve; sometimes we sell ourselves short. Sometimes the best philosophy is, *What do I got to lose?* It's about living your KPIs, leveraging your strengths, and seeing around corners. And you never know – it can even help win over that imposter.

———

Creative SCORE:
A Scientist at (He)Art

"Is it really creative, though? Your book was a good idea, but your most creative one...is it?"

From bread baking to mask making, from painting to gardening, the pandemic seemed to fuel human creativity. There is some research, in fact, that documents the relationship between the experience of crisis and emergence of creativity.[16] A profound sense of uncertainty, the kind that was brought on by the pandemic, can force creativity to emerge primarily because typical ways of being and customary ways of thinking are not as effective during a crisis. Creativity, in part, is a result of the necessity to foster the ability to cope. Many people turn to learn new skills or go back to revive old hobbies or reach out for any new experiences that can help them feel creative. This, in turn, can take minds off the imminent threats, generate a feeling of fun, and give a sense of accomplishment. Creativity, in essence, is a resource that can not only help find solutions to problems but also provide a sense of meaning and facilitate a new perspective.

Social scientists have proposed that creativity is one of the ways we can find meaning, in all its proposed dimensions – coherence, significance, and purpose.[17] Coherence here refers to the *ability to make sense of our lives*, significance as it relates to *seeing value in our being*, and purpose being the *sense of goals*. The COVID-19 pandemic upended lives in a very abrupt manner. In the same year, stark systemic inequalities were exposed – of the impact of the pandemic, the associated economic fallout, as well as with the social justice (re)awakening. It was a year that forced many to confront some very difficult truths. It is no surprise that it also forced us to look for meaning, and many turned to creative pursuits for a sense of well-being. My first book was published. It was certainly a meaningful creative pursuit. But it was not perceived as being *"really creative"* by my (adult) kids. *"Good idea"* but not my *"most creative."*

ART OF SCIENCE

An intense desire to be productive, with purpose, had led me to write a book. I compiled my essays into what is now the first book of the *Heart of Science* series,

---

[16]Tang et al., 2021. Creativity as a Means to Well-Being in Times of COVID-19 Pandemic: Results of a Cross-Cultural Study, Frontiers in Psychology, 12, 265.

[17]Kapoor, H. & Kaufman, J.C., 2020. Meaning-Making Through Creativity During COVID-19, Frontiers in Psychology, 11, 3659.

published by Society of Women Engineers (SWE) with all proceeds going toward a scholarship for underrepresented minority women in STEM. I thought it was pretty creative – the idea of writing a book, publishing it with SWE, and donating proceeds for a great cause. In the process, I learned about publishing, and I came up with creative ways of promoting the book. My kids were very proud of the effort it took, the unique way I brought it all together, and the cause, but they didn't think it was too much of a stretch. They thought that I had more creative in me. I worked through my defensive reaction, and upon some reflection, I realized that they might be right. Writing came naturally to me – I have been writing for as long as I can remember. In fact, if I hadn't been strongly encouraged to go for STEM education, I would certainly have been in humanities – a journalist perhaps, a very science-minded one at that.

Many people associate the word "creative" with artists, carrying the general assumption that art is more closely related to creativity than the sciences. Science and art are often thought to be quite unlike each other. However, many others contend that they can rely on a very similar creative process. Art and science also have many parallels when it comes to the cognitive skills and attributes required to create, to innovate, and to communicate the creativity of art and ingenuity of science. And the interplay of art and science can also lead to creativity. It is, unfortunately, something that isn't talked about or communicated much. In my view, creativity is very important in science. And I view science very creatively.

I love the art of science. I love the beauty of the scientific method, its mystery, drama, and intrigue. I live for the challenges and the satisfaction of finding relevant problems to solve and provide creative solutions that will help our customers. For me, it's like investigative journalism – *finding and uncovering information, asking a lot of questions, tracking down leads,* and *observing the clues.* I then like to stitch all the pieces of information together, like an artist, to develop a compelling narrative, like a storyteller, so I can convince myself and others that this is a problem worth solving. Then, it is about presenting the case, like a lawyer. I like to inspire others to join the cause and then, like expert craftsmen, work as a team on specific tasks, using the right tools to identify the building blocks needed to solve the problem. Then comes painting the vision of where to go next. The scientific method has an art to it, and its creativity inspires me to continually develop new concepts and newer ways of thinking, operating, and innovating. So, when is it that you are truly stretching on the paradigm of creativity? There was only one way to find out – I decided to dig deep into the science behind creativity.

SCIENCE OF CREATIVITY

Turns out, the concept of creativity has been the focus of much research since the 1950s.[18] Most experts recognize that creativity is not limited to those who happen to be highly recognized for their creative contributions. Important distinctions have been described among creative contributions, leading to a Four C model that was proposed to explore the construct of creativity.[19] The first of four aspects, *mini-c*, categorizes explorative behavior that may not necessarily be novel in a larger context, but is personally meaningful to the individual creator and tied to the process of learning. *Little-c*, or everyday creativity, comprises creative actions that most of us engage in on a regular cadence. The mini- and little-c creativities do not require any specialist status. *Pro-c* refers to expert-level creativity, but the expression may not have achieved eminence, yet. If and when Pro-c does achieve eminence, it can be considered to have progressed to the last category of *Big-C* creativity – significant eminence representing the peak of what can be achieved.

During the pandemic, we saw the Four C model for creativity play out.2 Mini-c and little-c behaviors were exercised at a personal level, oftentimes to facilitate coping, distraction, or amusement. Be it bread making or crafting, everyday creative activities were associated with a heightened sense of well-being and may have facilitated the deeper reflection experienced throughout the pandemic – the increasing frequencies mirroring accompanying uncertainties. With enough exposure and appreciation, some of these little-c activities may become Pro-c. Those who achieve eminent status as a result of their professional creative endeavors may possibly go on to reach Big-C with the passage of time. Overall, we have seen many examples of innovation and originality across all levels on the spectrum of creative accomplishment and ability. In fact, scientists (Pro-c) are an example – cited as frontrunners – who are at the cusp of Big-C eminence based on their response to the pandemic with creative contributions for developing vaccines against the novel coronavirus.

The world needs creativity – the world needs creative change. The pandemic has also shown us that we individually counted on our creativity to get through it. Many of us found our innate sense of creativity to keep us occupied, to entertain or help others, and to find our calling, in some cases. Creativity requires us to acknowledge its presence and take action. And when we do pursue it, our creativity manages to surprise us in creative ways. We need to harness this capability to shape the future.

---

[18] Beghetto, R.A. & Kaufman, J.C., 2007. Toward a Broader Conception of Creativity: A Case for "mini-c" *Creativity, Psychology of Aesthetics, Creativity, and the Arts*, 1(2), 73.
[19] Kaufman, J.C. & Beghetto, R.A., 2009. Beyond Big and Little: The Four C Model of Creativity, *Review of General Psychology*, 13(1), 1–12.

I had to dig deep to understand what would constitute a mini-c exploration for me during this unique time. And this is what led to *"Life is like a donut..."* taking life.

I had written these song lyrics over 10 years ago. In a serendipitous moment, I realized that the emotions and sentiments expressed in the words I had penned could truly represent the feelings of many during the pandemic. The lyrics needed to come alive in a song in my mind. And once the idea occurred to me, I couldn't get it out of my head, even though I wanted to not think about it. *It would be too hard to pull off!* I had virtually no connection with the musical arts, I barely listen to music, and I do not know musicians, nor did I have the faintest idea about what it takes to produce a song. I have an okay voice and can carry a simple tune. I don't consider myself a singer, I have no training, and I can't read music either. Armed with just the lyrics, I needed everything else – music, orchestra, singer, and a platform to put it out on.

Serendipity came to my rescue often during this creative project. Chance meetings and interactions played a strong role in bringing it to completion. I still haven't decided which of the 4Cs in my very own SCORE model should represent the C. The way I see it, all four got rolled into one. The *commitment* to see the project through was bolstered by *confidence* of pursuing many creative ideas in my day job as a scientist and driving them to conclusion despite not having the functional requirements in place at the outset. And that took *courage* here – to face my own fears and to venture out into uncharted territory. I was also intrigued by the *curiosity* to learn about a new area and approached it with open-mindedness. The scientist in me helped the budding artist.

I had to work up the courage to take personal risk. I also had to collaborate with people I had never met or interacted with before, which brought a sense of additional risk. But as is the case with my day job, commitment and enthusiasm for navigating this journey helped in influencing others to join along and collaborate on this new creative passion project. This was my mini-c. The **SCORE** at the heart of this song:

Serendipity

Commitment/Confidence/Courage/Curiosity

Open-mindedness

Risk-taking

Enthusiasm

"Life is like a donut...there'll always be a hole." 2020 may have created a void in our lives but, like the donut metaphor, this hole also serves to make us whole. We can

all step up and support each other. Hope for the future can fill our hearts as we find strength in solidarity. It could be the anthem the world needs. Maybe someday, a famous country singer will sing it. Maybe it would be Reba McEntire. Maybe it will be a Big-C. I won't hold my breath, but I knew I was being creative and stretching myself on this one. What I will hold on to are the reflections during the pandemic – of what we lost and what we seem to have gained.

Not everyone and everything is actively seeking to move up on the C scale, though. The concept of mini-c highlights how personal inspiration can be quite meaningful for the person. Researchers assert that finding meaning in creative expression is an adaptive response for building resilience to the stress induced by the pandemic. When faced with such existential crises, creativity not only increases but often tends to be directed toward establishing a legacy.

I should mention the incredulous look on my kids' faces when I told them what I was up to for my creative passion project. I was going to sing a song I wrote, and it could be downloaded with a donation. All funds would go to charity. *"Do you even know what you are talking about? How are you going to make this happen?"* They seemed worried that I would make a fool of myself...and embarrass them, I suppose. They even tried to talk me out of the idea.

It must be truly creative in that case! SCORE!

— FINE PRINT —

If someone told me there would be a song out there some day that I would have recorded based on a tune I composed, I would not believe it at all. *How or why would I possibly do a song?* But with the pandemic, many things changed – and we had to get creative and muster the courage to confront fear and self-doubt, to take risks, and be open to criticism, ridicule, or rejection.

Sometimes, we have to take that next step to see what we are capable of or what the moment demands of you. And before you go down this path, it is hard to anticipate the role serendipity plays. I even found the playitforward.com website serendipitously! I had an idea of what I needed – a website where I could upload my song, and as people downloaded and donated, the funds would be automatically directed to the charity that I would specify. I had been looking for such an option but hadn't come across any. And it just so happened that I caught a very moving segment in the news about a musician who lost his wife and wrote a song for his young son about his mother. He realized that any young kids who have lost parents may benefit from it, and all the proceeds from his song go to a charity that helps bereaved kids.

On a hunch, I followed up, and there it was – the website that could do exactly what I needed. I still find myself thinking, *How is it that, exactly when I was looking for this information, I happened to hear this story on the news?* Sometimes you only see things when you start down the path – you just have to believe and go for it. *You just have to get started.*

And I know this because I have often seen the same thing at work – we don't have all the answers, but we know what to question and things start falling together as we get going. The weak ties become stronger, the off-chance interactions become a lifeline, challenges are cracked, and barriers are broken.

And I have also found that a sense of purpose often helps in taking a leap of faith. That sense of purpose is what becomes the motivator and a protector, psychologically, and it also helps to bring others in. Many supported the song effort because it tapped into their sense of purpose, and they shared the vision. It happens at work as we drive our science to innovation to improve lives, and it did in this creative project. This experience also showed that, despite minimal opportunity for in-person communication, one can still be effective in communicating a sense of purpose and the vision. And this exercise has personally helped me in building my sense of creative confidence. We do need creativity at an individual level to help ensure that we will be creative as a society.

The project can be easily classified as a *failure* given that the song has not raised the kinds of funds I wanted to raise. It has been difficult to get the word out and there are so many worthy causes out there. But it will remain one of the highlights of the pandemic time for me because of all that I learned in the process of pursuing this idea and making it happen. I am so thankful to the musician who created the music and encouraged me to record in my own voice. I am thankful to my 3M colleagues who believed in this passion project of mine and lent me their support. I am thankful to my kids for raising my game, and my husband, and the United Way folks who kept encouraging me.

At the end of the day, this experience has taught me that it wasn't about how good my voice sounds but finding my creative voice.

———

"Life is like a donut..."[20]

Walked into the diner...and he sat down on a chair
Pain done smearin' on his face like chocolate on éclair
His skin was pale as mayo and empty was the stare
Eyes redder than ketchup...drippin' of despair
...n' circles of his eyes 'em looked like...big ol' coffee stains
His head in his hands he sat...and you could see the veins

Hurtin' he was doin'...had taken up its toll...n' I said...
Life is like a donut...there'll always be a hole

Life is like a donut...there'll always be a hole...
Somethin' that's a-missin'...and tuggin' at your soul
The pain that makes you all complete...is a part you don't control...
'Cause...life is like a donut...there'll always be a hole

The son who's out a' fightin'...the daughter you just lost
The mamma or yo' daddy gone when you needed them the most
The good friend in the wheelchair for no darn fault of his
The true love of your life that left...the one you're gonna miss
...n' the fire and the floodin'...from the stormin' and the rain
I seen 'em in here everyday...with every kind of pain

I say I hear ya baby...n' I say this to console...I say...
Life is like a donut...there'll always be a hole

Life is like a donut...there'll always be a hole...
Somethin' that's a-missin'...and tuggin' at your soul
The pain that makes you all complete...is a part you don't control...
'Cause...life is like a donut...there'll always be a hole

[20] ©2010 Jayshree Seth. Available on Play It Forward, https://www.playitforward.com/projects/344

Honey there's always somethin'...
We all gotta feel the sufferin'...
The hole right there it makes us whole...
So gotta go count your blessings...
Jus' livin' and lovin' and prayin'...
'Cause fixin' it can't be your goal...

Life is like a donut...there'll always be a hole...
Somethin' that's a-missin'...and tuggin' at your soul
The pain that makes you all complete...is a part you don't control...
'Cause...life is like a donut...there'll always be a hole...
Life is like a donut...there'll always be a hole

Survival MODES:
For Shore

"When we have hope, we discover powers within ourselves we may have never known... Once we choose hope, everything is possible."

— Christopher Reeve *(Superman)*

In many ways, 2021 felt like an extension of #2020, and these immutable words of the one who played Superman, with incredible powers, were a great reminder as we swam in different emotions. It appeared that even those with the most optimistic outlook were feeling somewhat worn down in early 2021. With the continued impact of the virus and its variants, amidst the news of ongoing trials and tribulations, and unrest and violence, there was an anticipatory feeling of yet another incoming wave of grief. As if, bracing in preparation, there was the slow slipping into the *"dulling of delight and dwindling of drive."*[21]

Typically, spring signals new beginnings, but 2021 began with a weary feeling of something old that was carried over, dampening the uplifting spirit of seasonal rebirth. Although there was good news on the vaccination front, challenges continued for many around the globe. The harsh reality of the delta wave of the pandemic and the havoc it wreaked on friends and family halfway across the globe were particularly distressing. All in all, the realization that 2021 just might continue to bear stark similarity to 2020 sank in deeper, for sure. And with that came the sense of treading water.

For me this sense was further heightened with the loss of a dear teammate. The untimely passing of a coworker is sad at many levels. For very close-knit teams, with a deep sense of personal connection and shared experiences, it is jarring. Losing someone that you had daily email exchanges and weekly meetings with, as you all row in unison toward a common goal, with immense focus and role clarity, is simply hard to accept at first. And with the pandemic, and the isolation it brought, the deep sense of grief is compounded and takes on a very different meaning. There is a sense of void that can perhaps only be filled by human presence, shared tears, and reassuring hugs. These go a long way in the journey toward acceptance and the coping process. In the absence of that, it can be difficult to find closure.

---

[21] Grant, A., "There's a Name for the Blah You're Feeling: It's Called Languishing," *The New York Times,* April 19, 2021.

NEVER IN A HUNDRED YEARS

Like many other aspects of our lives, the pandemic has reshaped the process of grieving, be it at home or work. It started out in 2020 with the weariness from the loss of mundane routines and then sadness at the loss of meaningful milestones and traditions – and grew to individual and collective grief as we heard of loss of lives and livelihoods, near and afar, further compounded with the world seemingly drowning three-deep in crises. The increasing rate of hate crimes throughout 2021 served as a reminder of the vulnerability of "others" in America – this time Asian Americans. And, with the virus raging again in many countries around the world, I heard of a friend suffering loss in their family too often. These were turbulent times in many ways.

In just a year, things that seemed quite inconceivable had normalized. The reality was that we were learning how to navigate through loss at a time when we were processing not just individual despair but also dealing with a sense of collective grief. Since time immemorial, humans have memorialized sad events with collective expressions of this grief. The tribe coming together helps share the sadness, strengthen memories, and fortify bonds. But now, we are having to find new ways of mourning and process our sense of loss.

Our work is a true team sport, and relationships matter as we advance science, build technology, and develop products. And grieve we did, with sobs, and tears, and stories shared over emails and texts and virtual meetings. We reminisced how often our late teammate was the recipient of our team's superman-cape rolling trophy, a fun team tradition, where the person who goes above and beyond gets the virtual cape image sent to them. The sense of loss will linger. And in many ways, we were forced to look inwards for the guiding light, the calm amid the turbulence around us, to stay grounded and navigate through this emotional storm, the severity of which was simply compounded because of the times and the accumulated toll they took.

YEAR ON YEAR...

For me personally, in order to deal with this wave of emotion, I had to dig deeper into what I had come to rely on based on my experiences in 2020. It was a year of reckoning, with tides of emotion, and then the intense desire to help and be productive, with purpose. Whether it was the global pandemic and its fallout, or the raw and real exposure of systemic racism on the world's stage, 2020 threw many of us off course. It was, however, also a year that should be credited for bringing into heightened focus many elements that we may have been somewhat blind to. It also led to a resolve to focus on issues that warrant more action, to dig deep into my own pockets of privilege to do something for others. After all, we all have some element of what may seem as "ordinary privilege." I took the time to remind myself and feel grateful for mine.

The concept of MEDS, an acronym for meditation or mindfulness, exercise, diet, and sleep, was critical during the pandemic for inculcating a sense of wellness.[22] I particularly have found peace in adding "O" to the equation with spending time outdoors, and going out for a brisk walk, every day, despite the weather. To wade through this latest bit of sad news, I relied heavily on these elements, processed at a deeper level...and I feel I was able to improvise and adapt as new understanding and strength emerged.

PLAY IT BY EAR

As I practiced these elements, a trip to the shores of Lake Superior made things crystal clear – my first overnight trip since the pandemic hit. Getting away and spending time in nature, the sense of awe and that connection to something bigger than ourselves, certainly helped in finding that *flow* again. Flow, as lead organizational psychologist Adam Grant called it – the *"antidote to languishing."*[21] I must admit, to counteract the languishing, it was best to also limit consumption of news and take time to starve despair and feed the soul instead. It kept me from constantly revisiting why things were the way they were. Sometimes, even for self-preservation, there is a need to throw a lifeline and let sleeping dogs lie.

With this awakening, I was able to immerse myself in another meaningful personal project that stretched my abilities. It filled my soul with a renewed sense of purpose and determination. This was the same sense I got when I was writing *Engineering Footprints, Fingerprints, & Imprints,* and the possibility it held in opening doors for others. And when I see that light, it helps me feel grounded again. For sure.

I see the deeper meaning behind the **MODES** for survival – shining a light over troubled waters.

> Mindfulness – *with gratefulness*
>
> Outdoors – *and open doors*
>
> Diet – *for mind and soul*
>
> Exercise – *ordinary privilege*
>
> Sleep – *and awakenings*

22 Kowalski, K., A Simple Wellness Strategy: MEDS (Meditation, Exercise, Diet, Sleep), SLOWW.co/meds, February 2019.

Also, there is now the slow realization that making a success of the innovation we were all working toward would be a great way to memorialize and honor our late teammate's commitment and effort. RIP.

"At some time, often when we least expect it, we all have to face overwhelming challenges. When the unthinkable happens, the lighthouse is hope. Once we find it, we must cling to it with absolute determination."[23]

After all, Superman said so.

— FINE PRINT —

They say grief comes in waves. The pandemic came in waves. The pandemic brought grief – in waves. The vaccines bring a wave of hope. The next wave of the pandemic brings anxiety – the news of boosters brings a wave of relief. It feels like we are hanging on – bracing for the next wave. And in between the waves of emotions that swept over us – we found ways to hang on.

Metaphors, I find them comforting and illuminating. I find them brilliant in their ability to take an abstract thought and transform it into a very physical, easily understandable, and often universal concept. They have a way of slipping into our language without us even consciously realizing it, as we attempt to describe our words, thoughts, or feelings. Social scientists propose that the human thought process is largely metaphorical, and metaphors can actively shape not just our language but our notions, emotions, and actions.[24] Metaphors can be literal, and they can be figurative. They can make a simple fact compelling as they add depth, character, and visual imagery. Metaphors can also help in alleviating negative feelings, and they are often associated with higher levels of emotional intelligence.

Some of us are find metaphors very moving and are motivated by inspirational quotes. And I am thankful to be among those, as it helps to process feelings, provide inspiration, and render meaning. Visiting Lake Superior was such an experience. The calm vast expanse of the lake looked like a mirror, as if urging reflection. And reflection helped with acceptance and a resolve for action. It not only brought vulnerability up to the

---

[23] Quote by Christopher Reeve
[24] Fetterman, A.K. & Robinson, M.D., 2014. What Can Metaphors Tell Us about Personality? *In Mind: the inquisitive mind, social psychology for you, 20.*

surface, but it also allowed me to get in touch with my deeper feelings of guilt and gratitude as I waved a mental goodbye. It also brought empathy for the many whose loved ones were lost and couldn't be mourned like we are accustomed to.

And the tall lighthouse, with its beacon beckoning weary travelers who may be adrift – it so encapsulated the pandemic grief compounded by the loss of our teammate. Mourning our friend's untimely passing was a dark moment, but there was light on the other side. There is no magic wand we can wave to make the grief disappear, and everyone will have their own individual and personal grieving process. In fact, when grieving, people often describe their sense of loss in metaphors. I know the still lake waters had a calming effect and the strong tall lighthouse helped build strength.

Grief and loss take on a different meaning in isolation, as we search deep within to find the power – to look for shore and the light – to look for hope.

————

SELF Reflection:
The Resolution Solution

"If you are not part of the solution, you are part of the problem..."

When my kids were young and they would complain about something, we would try to divert their thinking to finding solutions. Yes – so what can *we* do about it? Let's think about how we can solve this problem. The focus on solution was powerful in steering their thinking but so was the idea of using the word *we*. It signified to them that we acknowledge the issue and are willing to help in finding a solution, even though the problem may not impact us directly. We cared.

A memory that left an indelible impression on my young teenage self was a song by over 40 prominent artists who came together and created music history. "We Are the World," recorded on a January night in 1985, raised millions for famine relief in Africa. Back then, I didn't know many of the artists, but I recognized some from the Grammy Awards that were telecast for the first time in India in 1984. I have since read about how the project came together, and it is truly remarkable.[25] Despite their differences – in stature, in genre, and in styles – everyone was singing from the same song sheet. And, despite doubts and concerns, everyone wanted in on it because of the cause. It became a great example of doing something about a problem by using your skills, talents, and influence.

A DIFFERENT TIME

2020 was a problematic year to say the least, one that tore us apart literally and figuratively. As if a widespread pandemic of global scale along with political turmoil and social unrest weren't enough, there were many local and regional extreme climate events, wildfires, hurricanes, flooding, and droughts adding to an already tough year. In hindsight, the trouble had been brewing for a while, on all fronts, and whether it was the pandemic or social justice, or politics or climate change, it now served to crack the thin veneer, magnify our differences, and polarize our views. The year also brought about immense change, virtually overnight, as our lives at work, our work at home, and our home lives were concerned. Despite the few bright moments in the rising cacophony of crises, it was hard to reconcile the losses: the loss of security

---

[25] D'Agostino, "'We Are the World': Inside Pop Music's Most Famous All-Nighter," *Esquire*, June 24, 2020.

blankets, loss of civility and discourse, and the grave loss of lives and livelihoods. Let's just say it was a very different kind of year – one that perhaps warranted a break in the ho-hum resolution tradition.

SWAN SONG

Hindsight 20/20, it was also a year that led to tremendous reflection. It forced many of us to adjust to new priorities, examine our privilege, confront our biases, and acknowledge our roles in the crises that were unfolding. In many ways it forced a reckoning, as virtually all of us felt the individual anxiety, experienced collective grief, and grasped for eternal hope. Reflection also brought the gift of clarity in the midst of chaos, hope in the midst of despair – and the desire to live more mindful and meaningful lives. A desire to change for the better – to find common ground again. While 2020 upended our lives, we did adapt, practiced resilience, and continued reflection. Our isolation served to catalyze the cause for change at an individual, collective, and societal level.

In *Engineering Footprints, Fingerprints, & Imprints,* I wrote about that special time on New Year's Eve when it's the dusk of the year past and the impending dawn of the one just around the corner. I described how that brings along with it a desire to reflect, just in time for New Year's resolutions. In contrast, 2020 – almost in its entirety – gave ample opportunity for reflection. Many of the problems, exposed in a raw and real manner, were seeking solutions as we moved forward into a new calendar year against a backdrop of old tunes still in our heads and in our hearts. Who knew, at the time, the black swan year it would be? 2020 gets the CREDITS for revealing our blind spots through intense self-reflection brought on by the events. Many of these revelations require action from us with commitment, above and beyond typical New Year's resolutions that may or may not be adhered to past the first week!

SINGING PRAISES

A new beginning, like a new year, is perhaps a time to focus on being part of solutions to be made, over resolutions to be broken. There are at least four areas that many of us can agree on as being ripe for renewed commitment and immediate action given the crises we've faced: *science, social justice, sustainability,* and *solidarity.* Science has finally gained prominence in the eye of the public, and it requires continued support to deliver its potential on many fronts. The need for social justice was reawakened, and we need to rise up to the challenge. Sustainability and our relationship with the environment reside in a precarious position, demanding our attention. And, all these interconnecting elements are interwoven with the need for solidarity for our survival as humanity.

There is no denying the role of *science* and *technology* in keeping us together and in helping each one of us keep it together! Science, and the hope it inspired, was a trusted companion in the fight against the pandemic as we awaited the gift of science, in the vaccine. The global public was unified in the stance to follow the science as revealed by the results of 2020 3M SOSI. Digital technology allowed us to connect and communicate, to celebrate and commiserate, and to create and circulate like never before. However, the growing *science denialism* and rampant misinformation clearly show the need for change. It begs the question: How can we all, as individuals, play a part in the solution? For STEM professionals, it can be as simple as committing to engage in advocacy and amplifying science or encouraging students in STEM and participating in events. For others, it can be the commitment to seek out reliable sources, attend science communication events specifically designed for the public, or participate in citizen science platforms.

IN CHORUS

2020 was also the year that brought to the forefront the stark *equity* and *justice* issues as they related to the Black Lives Matter movement and the disproportionate impact of the pandemic on communities of color. Social science research shows that in order to address prejudice, one needs to spend time learning and understanding the people we perceive as being different from us and feel prejudiced against. It also calls for understanding the history and accepting past issues that may reflect the present circumstances. So, how do we contribute to building bridges? How can we all use our resources, our skills, time, talent, and influence to bring about much needed societal changes and shifts in attitudes? We can commit to learn, listen, and act to bridge the gap where disparities exist, whether in education, access, or health-care – to name a few – for all who are systemically denied opportunities, as well as those who feel disenfranchised. It starts with the recognition of the inequities, the commitment to our resolve to do something, and the willingness to do it. It could be as simple as marching, volunteering, donating, or acting in whatever capacity you feel you can to drive change. There is no cure-all formula or one-size-fits-all strategy.

The concept of stakeholder capitalism also gained momentum during the pandemic, emphasizing the need for *long-term resilience* and a *sustainable future*. There is ample evidence that connects our changing climate with the weather disasters we encountered in 2020. As organizations, companies, and governments move to prioritize de-carbonization and climate-related investments, what can we all do at an individual level? How do we all become part of the solution and take a more active role in caring for the planet and sustaining it for generations to come? This will involve a commitment to educating ourselves, to prioritize behavioral changes that can have a positive impact and influence our choices – especially since self-reflections in 2020 have made many realize that resilience, adaptability, and sustainability are going to be critical for our collective future on this planet.

WELL VERSED

Any action, in any of the above four issues, needs education, discussion, and strength of conviction as we read, reflect, and recognize the need for change. Another gift that 2020 did give us was finding strength and finding solidarity, and that should hold us in good stead – the strength that allowed us to survive the calamities that may have befallen us and to strengthen the conviction to cope. Cope with managing work from home and juggling schedules, maintaining strength to withstand loss of connections, jobs, resources, health – and at worst: loss of friends and loved ones. 2020 certainly challenged us, making it apparent that we are stronger when we work together by joining forces to collaborate and create community. We will need strength to find our voices and make them be heard, which may feel uncomfortable and will require us to draw on our collective strength.

WALK UP SONG

What we need, moving forward, is to put the focus on the word *solution* in *resolution*. I feel the need to commit to continue to reflect and act on how we can be part of solving these four key challenges, ones that seem complex but, in fact, will help us make headway because of their interconnectedness.

Yes, it's time to look in the mirror and focus on **SELF**, but a little differently than we might expect.

> Science and technology
>
> Equity and justice
>
> Long-term sustainability and resiliency
>
> Finding strength and solidarity

It's time to turn the *ME* into the *WE.*
It's time to take our individual reflections and turn them into actions for the collective good.
It's time to come together, yet again, because we are the world.
The time has come. WE – *is* the WORD.
I will be sharing my SELF.

— FINE PRINT —

As I casually shared my focus on SELF resolution with my kids, I braced myself for their reactions. I had a feeling that they would have thoughts and opinions. They seldom disappoint. First came the eye-rolls at another one of mommy's acronyms. I expect them – and I accept them.

"Are you virtue signaling?"

"I wouldn't know," I said and asked them to explain what that term meant. It was just like many other terms that I have had to learn recently, or rather, the context of those terms. I typically know the meaning of terms from reading about them if they have made it to the common vernacular; however, it is always good to hear the context my kids place a term within – especially given that we had a good discussion the week prior on the topic of "cultural appropriation." And, after some passionate arguments, we agreed to disagree on the distinction between cultural appreciation and appropriation, as well as the fine line in between. Not everything is as black and white as sometimes young minds tend to think it is – but their honest perspective often makes us reflect and question our own growing gray areas.

"Can you back it up?"

"Okay, back up – what do you mean back it up?" I asked.

"Can you back up your intention with action – because if you can't...you are just 'signaling' that you are 'virtuous.' Get it? It's what a lot of people do these days to put themselves into the conversation. You know... 'Look at me – I am so good. Look at me – what I am doing.'"

"Okay, but what if I genuinely want to help and am convinced it's the right thing to do?"

"Well...wanting and thinking don't achieve anything. That is actually 'performative activism.' You know, it's like posting a picture of yourself from a protest march to get likes. But you didn't do that – because you didn't join me in the march."

"Yes, I didn't – I told you I had my reasons. But I still support the cause in my own way. I support it in a way that works for me, for now. We all need to do what feels right to us. We agreed."

"Well...anyway...as long as you can show action. You know, many people and companies have been 'woke washing.' You know what that means right?"

I nodded.

"Okay, good, because you know that people who can't show action will get 'called out' or, worse yet, 'canceled.' You know what that means, right?"

I nodded.

"But what if I don't want to share my actions? Why can't I share my support and keep my actions private? I mean, isn't there a virtue to virtue signaling? Isn't it part of normal public discourse and our socio-psychological human makeup?"

"Is this going to be like our cultural appropriation discussion, Mommy?"

"No... I was just trying to understand why we are using a 'label' again and not considering its positives where there could be some."

"But what I don't understand is – if you are talking about social justice, why do you want to not talk about what you are actually doing to support it? Didn't you and Daddy start that fund and support minority students with your work? And don't your book sales go to a scholarship? Maybe it can inspire others to do something. I mean, if people buy your book, isn't it about them chipping in too?"

"Yes...that is how you turn 'me' to 'we'..." I mumbled.

"You do what? Okay, whatever. You do you, Mommy you do you."

I nodded.

Yup! No problem. *I'll focus on SELF*, I thought.

———

"Without reflection, we go blindly on our way, creating more unintended consequences, and failing to achieve anything useful."

– Margaret J. Wheatley,
It's An Interconnected World

SECTION 3

ACTION

*Power lies in action, the **karma**...*
with no fear of failure and no desire for fame.

STEM Echo-system:
Breaking Reflections and Reverberations...

Getting unstuck is not a given!

For many, perhaps nothing encapsulates 2021 like the image of the *Ever Given* stuck in the Suez Canal. For almost a week, we were seemingly mesmerized and watched the action unfold as the ultra-large container vessel (ULCV) got wedged horizontally in the narrow waterway, blocking the canal and halting all movement of billions of dollars of cargo. While the ship was stuck, the metaphorical memes flooded the internet. It was also a stark realization of what it really takes to get goods transported globally, including the risks and vulnerabilities in the system that were virtually hidden from the everyday consumer.[26] A single ship, an isolated event, brought about cascading impact. Global supply chains were still reverberating months later. No surprise, it even made it into common vocabulary to signify a situation or object(s) that slows or halts an operation that should have been preventable.

It took small ditch diggers, many excavators, and tugboats that were tiny in comparison, along with the help of tides, created by the gravitational tug of the moon, to finally get the stuck ULCV going again. In looking back, the *Ever Given* saga, and the effort to free it, also showed the strength of we, encapsulating the power of partnership – people working across the spectrum – across borders and sectors as allies, to find a solution for a problem that seemingly impacted us all. A ship that was stuck. Progress was driven by cooperation at an international level and spotlighted the importance of collaboration. Many of the problems that have (re)surfaced during the pandemic time have had far-reaching impacts, essentially requiring us to take action – build relationships, create kinship, and establish partnerships to arrive at solutions that stick.

SOUNDS GOOD

The ship did get stuck in 2021, but a lot was moving along as well. We entered 2021 with certainty that it would be rife with uncertainty, unlike 2020 which delivered a shock we weren't prepared for. As the vaccines started rolling out, there was a heightened sense of optimism thanks to vaccines, which were developed and could

[26] Braw, E., "What the *Ever Given* Taught the World," *Foreign Policy.* November 10, 2021.

be made available due to game-changing partnerships and shared action across the stakeholder spectrum resulting in significantly shortened timelines. Given the crisis, there was in some cases, unprecedented levels of sharing and collaboration. It occurred globally between manufacturers, governments, academia, and research institutions with the shared goal of accelerating the innovation, qualification, registration, and dissemination of vaccines to the global public.

On a personal front, I was finally able to travel to India to visit family after two long years. This was only possible because of cooperative "Transport Bubble" arrangements created based on equalization of risk of infection between the country where the journey started and the destination country. These reciprocal partnerships established between specific countries eliminated the need for quarantine and self-isolation. This was critical to maximize our time with family, minimize logistical issues, and reduce the risk of getting stuck on arrival or on the way back.

SOUNDING OFF

As vaccination rates went up and restrictions eased, I accepted my first out-of-town invitation to speak. I had the privilege of delivering the Annual Silas Lecture, in-person, at Georgia Tech. A series that focuses on ethics and leadership as essential components of an engineering education, I got the opportunity to talk about the state of science and the need for STEM advocacy. It is clear from the results of 3M SOSI, ongoing academic research, and empirical evidence that there has been a convergence of many issues such as diversity, equity, and inclusion (DE&I), social justice, sustainability, and their confluence with STEM and its advocacy. In my role as Chief Science Advocate, I have had the opportunity to listen, learn, and lead through interactions with members from the entire stakeholder spectrum of the STEM ecosystem.

It is important for students to think about the decisions and choices that they will make as they step out in the world – as educators, entrepreneurs, employees, or employers. A diverse workforce is a robust and resilient workforce, and it makes economic as well as moral and ethical sense. Increasing diversity also lends itself to a more positive sentiment around science and more loyalty among socially conscious customers. Single-minded views of meritocracy can promote undue focus on the individual and a loss of social context as a result. Students need to develop an empathetic lens, be able to see their own privilege, and contribute to alleviating inequities – *it's the right thing to do.*

I have often written about the primary challenges underrepresented minorities face across the STEM spectrum, from early childhood, K-12, and higher education all the way to the workplace. These challenges can range from simple knowledge gaps about potential career opportunities to the lack of role models and representation that can limit aspiration and inspiration to pursue STEM. For others, it may be the limited financial means to support a STEM education, or it may be minimal support and guidance that limits opportunities as students navigate their educational journey. And for others who are marginalized in STEM, it may be the explicit discrimination and implicit biases at work that have them stuck.

There are metaphorical blockages along this spectrum that deter substantive change, resulting in trickle-down effects that contribute to issues like the "leaky pipeline." The question remains: How can we get these obstructions unwedged and unstuck for sustained momentum and sustainable changes? These will certainly not dissolve on their own and work themselves out – they require collective action. The solution involves complex, multifaceted issues with multiple stakeholders including parents, teachers, educators, mentors, peers, and employers with a strong role of family, schools, community, society, and culture across the key elements of this E'co-system:

· Exposure · Encouragement · Empowerment · Education ·

· Economics · Engagement · Equity ·

SOUND IT OUT

The world requires innovation. Innovation needs science. Science demands diversity. Diversity warrants equity. Moving forward, it is imperative that there is a better understanding of the issues and solutions for each of the above elements of this spectrum. Environments that lack diversity are closed communities that have been called analogous to echo chambers where the same voices continue to reflect and reverberate, and the problem sets are identified with a very narrow point of view. A narrow perception of excellence results in a narrow cross-section of well-represented scientists getting the bulk of resources and recognition. 3M 2020 and 2021 SOSI results indicate that there is an urgent need for a broader perspective and social context for science by building a more diverse science community and science as a more inclusive space. A narrow view also makes science vulnerable.

This topic is discussed at length in a recent landmark paper that was co-published in several leading science journals.[27] The authors propose a redesign of performance and promotion evaluation systems to include the accomplishments of those who serve as champions of change through outreach, DE&I efforts, and

---

[27] Urbina-Blanco et al., 2020. A Diverse View of Science to Catalyse Change, *Journal of the American Chemical Society*, 14(34), 14393-14396.

mentoring of marginalized scientists – they believe it is integral to excellence in modern science, and that these criteria will build more accountability and have a positive outcome. And 'til that happens, the reverberations that often do not reflect the diversity of the scientific community continue – the echos of a community which itself does not reflect the diversity of society as a whole.

Science has given solutions to dampen sound reflections and reverb. These involve adding carpets and rugs on the floor, porous fabric or open-cell foam panels along the walls, or furniture to the area to absorb the sound.

The same strategy can be a metaphor for DE&I in STEM to make more room:

Support from ground up: *Facilitate diversity*

Open-mindedness all around: *Foster inclusion*

Seats at the table: *Further equity*

SOUNDING BOARD

The importance of the above S.O.S. strategy also surfaced in my interactions with Dunwoody School of Technology when I had the privilege of keynoting at the Annual Kate Dunwoody 2021 Luncheon. It is an event that raises funds, celebrating the power of scholarships and the impact they can have in helping women pursue a degree in technical education. There was much discussion on factors that may influence participation of underrepresented students in STEM and skilled trades. These include intrinsic factors and external/environmental factors from an early age, with familial, cultural, and social influences as well as academic mindsets and attitudes. But for many, it is primarily a matter of economics, and helping bridge that gap is critical.

For those who are fortunate to receive scholarships and financial assistance, there are still barriers that are often encountered as recipients enter educational institutions. The need for interventions that reduce or eliminate these barriers is increasingly recognized as a critical aspect of access for students in STEM.[28] In addition to increasing institutional accountability, understanding resource disparity, and creating strategic partnerships, experts recommend curriculum adjustments to truly connect with student creativity through community-based learning opportunities, and/or by finding ways to emphasize how classroom content relates to prosocial communal outcomes.

This topic is of specific interest to me, and I am excited to have initiated collaboration with Professor Amanda Diekman's group, at Indiana University, to

[28] Estrada et al., 2016. Improving Underrepresented Minority Student Persistence in STEM, *CBE – Life Sciences Education,* 15(3), es5.

understand how facing challenges affects students' perceived goal opportunities in their majors. We want to understand communal goal affordances and interventions that can help minority students persist in STEM. Particularly, the perceptions that STEM careers lack opportunities to connect with others and conduct work that benefits others (i.e., communal goals), which may decrease interest in pursuing a STEM career.

After a year that felt stuck in many ways, I am hopeful that "allyship" can get many a thing moving – and lead to mindful action and meaningful change.

— FINE PRINT —

I have newfound appreciation for the word allyship – *the central idea that you can advocate, support, and show solidarity for a group that you are not a member of.* I feel like it has elements of leadership, relationship, and partnership rolled into it. The leadership of proactive action, not just thoughts, prayers, or words – but action. Actions of educating oneself, recognizing one's own privilege and bias, and then exercising that awareness to act for equity. It requires building of trusting relationships with those who may not have had the same lived experience as you. It is the realization that partnerships for a common purpose make us powerful and help in dismantling the power dynamics that may disadvantage or advantage others.

We have seen what we can achieve with collective action, collaboration, and cooperation as it plays out on the world's stage. We do need more of it. We also need more allyship at an individual level. It may seem like a tough ask – *to acknowledge a power structure and give up power.* But true allies drive lasting change. In an organizational setting, they can help to address numerical underrepresentation and negative stereotyping that can stack the system against those who have been marginalized, with a lasting impact throughout their careers. Allies recognize that those who are underrepresented may experience greater performance pressure because they are fewer and so highly visible. Minorities also carry the tremendous responsibility of becoming mentors and role models to others, which impacts their time with demands and contributions that the mainstream majority needs to appreciate and truly understand.

We certainly need allyship in STEM – we talk a lot about the need for men to be allies for the cause of gender equity. Men in leadership positions need to recognize that there can be more discrimination, harassment, disparity in pay, and social isolation for women in STEM and act to change it. They have to be allies in recognizing and stamping out microaggressions. Given that STEM fields often have such a male context, it may lead others to think: How can anyone else possibly be good at science? It can hit the very identity – *Can I really be a scientist?* – and this internal tussle can lead to psychological distress. Intersectionality further adds to the complexity for women of color or those who identify as non-binary. Allies attempt to understand, empathize, and act.

In my experience, very few men show up at *women's events* – events meant for all, but only those who identify as women typically show up. True allies know that showing up does help, speaking up helps more, and standing up in action really matters. But I have also come to believe that there is tremendous value in women's events because strong identification with others in the community helps increase a sense of belonging and inclusion, fostering a sense of mentorship and social support. It can promote a sense of voice, and it creates this mechanism where one can express feelings, share experiences, and hear the challenges others face. I have seen how it can serve to build courage, bolster confidence, and create a sense of one's own agency and empowerment. It gives a platform to brainstorm strategies, network, and support one another. It has also helped me personally in understanding the many issues faced by others that I may have never even thought of, let alone face.

The desire to be an ally forces me to reflect upon my own privilege, in all its intersectionality, and continue to progress in the journey of allyship, across the spectrum – gender and gender expression, race, orientation, ethnicity, disability, age, etc. Understanding my own capacity to use time, talent, money, and heart has allowed me to share from my pockets of privilege to advance underrepresented minority women in STEM. I hope it will make me a better ally for other causes as well, which in turn I can use to impact organizational change and contribute to collective action in steering the ship in the right direction – *by taking action.*

The key to getting *unstuck* is allyship – the dictionary.com word of the year for 2021!

———

The Right Angle:
Cutting on the BIAS

"Geez, Mommy...you need to stop saying, 'Hey, guys!'"

Words evolve, in that their usage changes as our world evolves, and the meaning they signify can be quite different than the origins. Such is the case with the word *guys*, which enjoyed a transition from a negative connotation to a fairly positive reference and then to a generic word. But many believe that the use of guys to address mixed-gender groups still reinforces androcentric bias and validates male privilege. Despite what the dictionary asserts, many disagree with the use of male-generic terms that seemingly position men as the default.[29] This can specifically be an issue in male-dominated fields – *the speaker's intent may be to address everyone but those listening may not necessarily perceive it as so.*

Research shows that gender-exclusive words and language can impact a person's sense of belonging, motivational drive, and even career aspirations.[30] In fact, male-gendered wording in job descriptions has been shown to have an effect on how certain jobs are perceived and the appeal they hold, thereby impacting the very likelihood of women applying for them. After all, language often reflects culture and gives insights into societal norms. Additionally, it shapes thought, neural pathways, and psychological constructs. It wields the power to reinforce dominance and exclude marginalized groups. But others have questioned, among the litany of issues as they relate to the world of diversity in STEM, how concerned we should be with this one word, or others like it.

After reading and reflecting, I have come to believe that the words and terms we use must speak to an inclusive environment, especially as we look to dismantle systemic barriers and reimagine societal constructs, armed with the reawakening during the last two years. Casual words may be a miniscule factor, but many small elements can add up to create big hurdles when viewed from a diversity angle. The use of words like guys can mainstream male presence and marginalize the participation of others. Language can impact perceptions, and language can guide decisions that add to unconscious bias – any way you cut it.

[29] "'You Guys': Is There A Better Option?" *Dictionary.com*, December 19, 2018.
[30] Gaucher, D., Friesen, J., & Kay, A.C., 2011. Evidence That Gendered Wording in Job Advertisements Exists and Sustains Gender Inequality, *Journal of Personality and Social Psychology*, 101(1), 109.

DIVERSE ANGLES

Unconscious, or implicit, bias deserves much attention as it continues to impede women's success despite measures being taken to address explicit bias against women. The explicit measures are often clearly instituted to encourage involvement, enhance participation, and advance women's careers. However, unconscious bias is harder to detect, acknowledge, and manage because it can influence perceptions without one recognizing its existence. With active legal means, leadership measures, and DE&I initiatives in place to create a level playing field, it appears unconscious bias is the *next frontier* because it can have the same impact as conscious bias and the same damage. Unconscious bias permeates society and continues to impact gender inequality in professional settings, especially in STEM fields. So, it is important to study causes, consequences, and control strategies of both conscious *and* unconscious forms of gender bias.

Additionally, we need to consider the unintended reinforcement of the gender binary that emerges as we work to establish space for women. People are increasingly expressing themselves beyond conventional gender norms and archetypes, reclaiming traditions and paving new paths. Those who identify as gender non-conforming experience much of what women encounter within the limitations of gender bias, while *also* being obstructed by the construct of the binary itself. As we lead the way for addressing implicit bias, we have to be cognizant of gender diversity and the evolution of its social constructs within our society.

A lot has changed in the last two years, including the public perception of science and what the public feels are imperatives as we move forth. 3M SOSI results show that there is a heightened recognition of the importance of diversity in STEM and in many ways the realization that science can be the most impactful if diversity is reflected in those who learn, teach, and practice science. Diversity helps to ensure a wider lens on problems to solve, a more comprehensive reflection, and a better view of the solution set. There is ample research to show that heterogenous teams are more likely to arrive at innovative solutions. These solutions are perhaps more likely to gain wider acceptance owing to that diversity.

INCLUDED ANGLES

Bias training that stops at simply explaining the science behind bias and the simplistic downside of discrimination fails to achieve results. A recent paper equated such efforts to a weight-loss program that told participants to step on the scale and basically left it at that. [31] It is imperative that training programs

---

[31] Gino, F. & Coffman, K., "Unconscious Bias Training That Works," *Harvard Business Review*, September-October 2021.
[32] Project Implicit, https://implicit.harvard.edu/implicit/takeatest.html

raise awareness and teach strategies to manage bias and measure progress. Many organizations include assessments through the Implicit Association Test[12] after educating on the need for training and the explanation of the terms and the supporting science. Storytelling, testimonials, and play-acting are also powerful strategies to make people aware of biases and how they can play out.

The downside of check-the-box-type training on complex topics, such as unconscious bias, is the inability to make lasting change. There is a widespread recognition that hiring of diverse candidates is not good enough – we need to work to make the working environment more inclusive as well. Workplaces are taking notice, and many are responding by including training programs, creating taskforces, implementing top-down initiatives, and mobilizing grassroots efforts to make work environment more diverse, inclusive, and equitable. A longer-term commitment to eliminate bias is reflected in the attempts to change not just recruitment strategies but reflected in structural, procedural, and cultural changes to marketing campaigns, performance appraisals, promotion protocols, and reward systems, to name a few. This includes the most egregious and overt examples of bias, such as being sensitive to terms, words, and language being used, as well as the subtle exclusion or undermining of contributions that are typically the most prevalent and harmful forms of bias.

EQUAL ANGLES

The Implicit Association Test is an eye-opening tool that demonstrates we can all be equally influenced by unconscious bias as we make automatic associations that come, top of mind, between certain traits and certain groups. It is a rapid speed sorting task that measures the degree of overlap a person sees between concepts (e.g., "scientist" and "male" or "nurse" and "female"). A simple tool that makes people see their own bias can make them mindful, while also offering the opportunity to understand why others may have it. These tests are powerful because most people deny they are biased, and it is hard to address bias if people don't accept that they have it. The test shows that bias is a normal psychological trait, but not unavoidable, and acting on it to the detriment of others is unacceptable.

The recognition of bias in one's own self can help people have better receptivity to a combination of strategies for overcoming bias. Among those listed by Gino and Coffman[11] include: "calling out stereotyped views" through everyday examples, relying on more "individualized information about people" versus broad generalizations based on their background, "reflecting on counter-stereotypical examples" that can serve to reduce prejudice, "adopting the perspectives of others" to understanding how bias may be at play, and "increasing [interpersonal] interactions with different kinds of people" with a sense of open-mindedness.

Highlighting examples of women leaders who are successful in traditionally male roles can show that there are indeed ways for everyone to succeed in the organization. Reframing a situation or person is a powerful technique as well. Instead of making judgments about someone's background or style, figuring out how it could be an asset instead allows for growth. Having leaders discuss and reflect upon experiences where they believe they may have operated in a biased manner sets an example. This helps others examine their own biases and reflect upon factors that may have shaped their views.

WORKING THE ANGLES

After a facilitated screening of the 3M docuseries Not The Science Type, launched in 2021, much of the panel discussion focused on audience questions around convincing organizations regarding the value of diversity, and helping management be more conscious of unconscious bias. In my simplistic view, we need to address it from all angles: we need corporate values, we need leaders talking about the importance of these corporate values, and if we can have metrics that connect to these values, they also help to drive management behavior. But, at the end of the day, it comes down to each one of us to understand, monitor, and cut down instances of bias to positively impact the culture we stitch together.

So, I shared the way I like to think about it:

- **Speak up:** When you witness bias, address it, respectfully.

  We need to address bias, *don't stay silent when you notice it.* And, by the same token, we need to be okay with people pointing out something we may be doing (such as using the word "guys" in a mixed-gender meeting). Giving feedback in a work setting takes courage, especially when it involves hierarchical relationships, but in my experience, people welcome such feedback that can make them more effective. Sometimes we just don't know what we don't know, and someone helping us correct something that we may be doing is incredibly valuable. When we give feedback, it takes courage to confront fear of reprisal and the risk of being ostracized. On the flip side, when we receive feedback, it takes courage to be thankful, as hard as it may seem in the moment.

- **Check in:** Reach out to people, casually.

  I have come to really value the power that informal conversations and hallway chats hold in a work setting. It's the one-to-one connections with people you work with that allow us to get to know each other and develop trust – trust to be able to share concerns as they arise, and trust to give and receive feedback when warranted. With remote and hybrid work modes, it is getting more and more difficult to run into people and check in casually. We need to find ways to recreate these touchpoints. I have made it a practice to send a note to anyone who is a subject of an announcement – job changes, promotions, retirements – *even if I didn't know them personally*. We need the little things that connect us to each other as humans and create common understanding. And again, it goes both ways – share and let others share to foster relationships and build trust.

- **Venture out:** Connect with people outside your immediate circles, regularly.

  I am also noticing that as our days get packed with back-to-back online meetings with our immediate work teams, it is harder to engage in the other activities that were easier to participate in when we were in-person. For example, at 3M, we often gathered for celebrations and events organized by our employee affinity groups, engaged in local community projects, and interacted at poster sessions promoting our 15% culture. All these interactions facilitated new touchpoints with people outside the immediate work group, and associations with people we wouldn't necessarily meet – *from different functions and backgrounds, with different roles and perspectives*. It is now more important than ever to find ways to venture out of the comfort zone to break what I've described previously as the *sound of silos*. It may not feel comfortable at first, but oftentimes that sense of discomfort becomes a motivation for introspection and examining of our own bias.

- **Pin down:** And finally, question your own biases.

  Implicit bias is difficult to identify, and it's also very hard to admit to owning it, despite the fact that we all have it. We may also be unaware of the impact it has on others. Accessing the network of younger folks is actually a great exercise that can help with self-reflection, pinning down bias and identifying what shaped our worldviews and how they need to evolve. My *Gen Z* kids have been instrumental in helping me adjust my *mental* models. It is important to do some reflection to figure out our own areas of bias and assumptions that are creeping into our judgment.

I find that this *in-out, up-down* framework can allow us to get a 360-degree view of the topic. It positions us at an angle where we can start seeing how small actions can help transform the work culture to become more inclusive. When combined with organizational efforts, we can truly see how diversity and commitment to equity flourishes in such an environment. We all need **BIAS** for action:

Be vocal, stay vigilant

Initiate informal interactions

Access other associations

Self-assess and self-monitor

It's not the words alone but the actions too that matter. Gendered language can certainly reinforce stereotypes and hinder diversity, but an environment of mutual trust – where everyone is willing to give feedback, engage with others, and examine one's own bias – can go a long way in ensuring a more inclusive environment for guys, gals, and gender-nonconforming people.

You can take my word for it.

— FINE PRINT —

Yes, I have stopped using *guys*. But I must admit I pushed back with data when my daughter first pointed out that I was using the word guys to address a mixed-gender group. Denial of bias is a typical first reaction. I explained to her the origin of the term and the current neutrality that convinced me it was okay to use. I even argued that there was no alternative term that can easily be used instead of guys, contending that there is no plural word that appropriately addresses the space the word guys has come to occupy in our colloquial vernacular. But her point was that my using the word guys normalizes the male default and might have a negative impact. The motivation to change wasn't for the benefit of those who may not think anything of the word, *but for those who may feel it as yet another word that reminds them that they don't belong.*

"Hey, folks." "Hey, y'all." "Hey, team." I have used them all since, but sometimes I am at a loss for words. And I often speak up and suggest we refrain from using it when I hear others using it. I share the story about my daughter asking me if I would ever consider using "Hey, gals" to mixed-gender groups and what the reaction would be. Listening and learning from feedback is a key to correcting bias and becoming more inclusive. Sometimes we just don't know what we don't know, and someone helping us correct something that we may be doing is incredibly valuable.

But it's hard. And I must admit, even given my personality and my position, I have been reticent about giving feedback. For instance, I had a peer who felt the need to explain what I had just said to the group at every meeting. I could tell they felt they were helping, and I didn't want to share how it made me feel – I was the only woman in that group. Perhaps if they had asked for feedback, I would have shared. Knowing that, I have often resorted to specifically asking for feedback after my own presentations or tough meetings and interactions. We all make mistakes.

I also reach out for feedback to extend my network beyond those I already know. I find myself much more active on exchanging texts and messages and connecting with people on random topics to foster connections. It's not enough to see people through a screen in formal meetings to develop the trust and understanding needed for feedback and open discussions. And I have noticed that, even in work meetings, it is getting much easier to post negative feedback, anonymously, which oftentimes may not have the desired positive impact.

Outreach efforts outside of our immediate work unit serve to mix it up and allow engagement with different ideas that make us think and grow in unexpected ways. For instance, I try to attend as many DE&I events at work as I can, especially the ones that invite inspirational speakers from around the world to address our 3M community, or ones that facilitate diverse employees getting together and coordinating an event or completing a project. I also attend events in my role as Chief Science Advocate that bring me together with communities I typically don't have access to. After such interactions, I feel appreciation of others' lives and the challenges they may face, as well as an interest in their welfare. Interacting with diverse networks creates new associations and relationships that can serve to raise awareness and contribute to reducing bias, stereotypical impressions, and prejudice.

I try to examine my own biases as well. I recall a particular instance where a simple scanning of the leading thinkers I follow on LinkedIn really made me think about the implicit bias that had directed me to follow a very narrow demographic cross-section. I took action to diversify the list and reached out to be included in more diverse networks, openly admitting that I had been implicitly influenced. Once I acknowledged and questioned it, I realized it's not possible that all leading management thinkers have one homogenous identity. There is more work to do. And of course, my adult kids are very vocal about giving me feedback on my views, my style, and the way I come across – *under the guise of helping me.*

CAST-off Characteristics:
Not the Science Type

Who is the "science type?"

If the Draw-a-Scientist social experiment first conducted in the '60s with elementary school children in the U.S. and Canada is any indication, back then, it was certainly a man.[33] Out of the almost 5,000 scientists drawn by the children who participated in the experiment, only 28 drew a female scientist. All of those were drawn by girls and not a single boy drew a woman. Progress has since been made – it is very promising to see that as gender roles in society evolve so do children's imagination of what is possible. But we are not close to parity yet. In recent decades, on average, 28 percent of the children drew female scientists. Interestingly at age 6, girls draw 70% of scientists as women, but by the time they are 16, they draw around 75% of scientists as men, with the number starting to flip at around 10 years of age.

Much research has been done on the topic of why many girls and young women do not see themselves, or even their gender, in science careers. A multitude of factors can contribute to this at an individual, group, cultural, and societal level. Studies have found that a less pronounced masculine image of science has the potential to increase the likelihood of STEM career aspirations.[34] Among strong factors that dissuade girls are the characteristics that have become associated with the people who pursue STEM education and the construct around the realities and perceptions of education and careers in these male-centric fields. This resonates. I wouldn't have opted for STEM – *thinking that I too was not the science type.* I am fortunate that my unique circumstances prompted that I nonetheless pursue STEM, and here I am today – a corporate scientist – the highest level at 3M and an advocate for STEM in my role as our first-ever Chief Science Advocate.

CAST A LIGHT

Sharing our personal stories can be an incredible mechanism for illuminating the data with the power of anecdote. Though it required stepping outside of my comfort zone, I was honored to be among the female scientists highlighted with the launch of *Not the Science Type,* a docuseries featuring my story and that of nuclear engineer Dr. Ciara Sivels, microbiologist Dr. Jessica Taaffe, and STEM innovator

---

[33] Yong, E., "What We Learn From 50 Years of Kids Drawing Scientists," *The Atlantic,* March 20, 2018.
[34] Makarova, E., Aeschlimann, B., & Herzog, W., 2019. The Gender Gap in STEM Fields: The Impact of the Gender Stereotype of Math and Science on Secondary Students' Career Aspirations, *Frontiers in Education,* 4, 60. 109.

Gitanjali Rao. We have all confronted bias or discrimination as we pursue our chosen STEM fields. And while each one of us has taken a different path to pursuing scientific excellence, we are bound by the common experience of feeling not the type for a multitude of reasons like racial, gender, or age-related bias. While we may not have always thought of ourselves as the science type, now we feel the need to share our insights and advocate for equity in science. The series was created in order to spark a deeper conversation about stereotypes and their negative impact on STEM diversity, equity, and inclusion.

This topic is especially important, as we need all the diversity we can muster to creatively solve the challenges we face as a society such as global healthcare issues and climate change – just to name two. If STEM fields are viewed in a negative light, it will certainly dissuade girls *and* boys from pursuing such interests. As a result, public awareness and appreciation of science can suffer, which in turn can lead to loss of funding at all levels. Science is critical to our future. Scientific fields need adequate representation, not just in order to innovatively solve problems, but also to ensure that we arrive at solutions that work for all. In fact, 2021 results of 3M SOSI show that the world recognizing diversity can help science achieve more, including greater global collaboration between scientists, more innovative ideas, new and improved approaches to existing research techniques, and more research and innovation to help underserved populations.

CAST ASIDE

Given that most of the STEM fields were largely laid out by men for men,[35] there are many systemic barriers that women who do enter the field still confront, as they often have to navigate the onlyness along these established and entrenched pathways. They encounter systems that often have little reason or motivation to change, given the majority. The award-winning documentary *Picture a Scientist* spotlights issues such as the overt discrimination and subtle microaggressions women face. Also, there are behavioral norms and expectations, skills and styles, tokenism, and typecasting that can all seemingly promote gendered barriers, further stacking the system against women and impacting them disproportionately throughout their careers. Adding certain evolutionary psychological traits and powerful social conditioning to the mix, systemic experiences with discrimination can lead to lower satisfaction levels and it can chip away at confidence. Intersectionality further compounds these issues – *many female and gender-nonconforming scientists simply take themselves out of the science picture.*

---

[35]Cyr, E.N. et al., 2021. Mapping social exclusion in STEM to men's implicit bias and women's career costs, *PNAS*, 118, 40.

It's not just the school or college or work environment, *it's even ingrained into the way we teach, typify, train, track, and talk about STEM.* I often speak about the importance of context as a critical aspect of science that engages underrepresented populations, as opposed to the content-only approach that has been traditionally used. In fact, a 2008 study from the National Academy of Engineering asked students if they wanted to be engineers.[36] No surprise – girls were twice as likely to say "no." But, when the context of what engineers *do* became the backdrop of the question – such as: Who would like to design a safe water system? Who would like to save the rainforest? – it was a resounding "yes" from girls.

I have previously mentioned how I, myself, didn't see the connection of STEM careers to my pro-social goals. When you are young, you may often need someone to make these connections for you. I know I did. A change in the construct, with addition of rich context, is an intervention that will serve to inspire young girls and underrepresented minorities to pursue STEM – before the die is cast in middle school.

CAST A WIDER NET

In addition to the construct of the field and the stereotypical portrayal of science, there are also the deep-rooted gender stereotypes that can impact a child's social identity and the perception of who is a scientist and who can be a scientist. Not only do girls not see themselves in these roles, stereotypes also have prejudicial effects on how boys view women in STEM roles when they encounter them in real life. Furthermore, popular culture archetypes of *scientists as dispassionate villains, maverick heroes, nerdy geeks, socially awkward, and loner stereotypes* are all often incompatible with the way girls see themselves. These portrayals serve to lessen the appeal of science itself. There may be positive stereotypes as they relate to genius scientists with exceptional skills, but it essentially serves to replace one stereotype with another.

There has been a lot of effort to portray women and gender nonconforming adults in STEM so more people can envision themselves pursuing STEM education and succeeding in STEM careers. Role models in science careers ("STEM Gems"), exposure to the kinds of careers there are, and adequate representation of women in science curriculum can be effective strategies to combat stereotypes. This can also counteract the impact of stereotypes that serve to limit a student's self-confidence,[34] discourage STEM engagement,[37] and widen the achievement gap.[38] In order to encourage more girls to pursue STEM education and more women to persist in

[36] National Academy of Engineering. 2008. *Changing the Conversation: Messages for Improving Public Understanding of Engineering.* The National Academies Press.

[37] Ertl, B., Luttenberger, S., & Paechter, M., 2017. The Impact of Gender Stereotypes on the Self-Concept of Female Students in STEM Subjects with an Under-Representation of Females, *Frontiers in Psychology.* 8, 703.

[38] Appel, M. & Kronberger, N., 2012. Stereotypes and the Achievement Gap: Stereotype Threat Prior to Test Taking. *Educational Psychology Review,* 24(4), 609-635.

STEM careers, we need to **CAST** off these characteristics associated with science, and scientists, that hinder the engagement, participation, and success of women in these fields:

Constructs

Archetypes

Stereotypes

Typecasting

There has never been a better time to change the constructs and shatter these images! The pandemic has ignited a renewed interest in STEM careers and education. More than half of the respondents of 3M SOSI in 2021 say that the pandemic is inspiring a new generation to pursue science-based careers, and the public agrees girls and women in STEM still face obstacles relating to their gender. Moreover, seven in ten people around the world agree – there are negative consequences to society if the science community fails to attract more women and girls.

Not the Science Type was produced to inform, influence, and inspire. We hope our series provokes more conversation on this topic. And I hope it leads to more action toward developing effective strategies for engaging more girls and retaining more women in STEM. It is my hope also that those who see the docuseries realize that there are many paths, myriad prospects, and multiple perspectives – you don't have to be a specific race or gender or ethnicity or nationality, you don't have to be a child who tinkered, and you don't have to have a degree – *to be the science type!* It shows that our paths can be diverse, just as diverse as we all are, and science will be better off for that diversity. You can bring in your interests, shape your roles, and pursue your passions – and you can blaze trails with *potential that is exponential.*

— FINE PRINT —

It is quite a surreal feeling to see your story being told on a big screen – only eight minutes, but plenty of time to run through the gamut of emotions. I laughed, I winced, and I held back tears during the Tribeca premiere, reminding myself of the makeup I had on my face. The amygdala had been activated with words and images that are certainly triggers for my brain – *parents, friends, family – reliving the trials and tribulations and joys and celebrations of the past.* Parts of my identity, not typically visible, were laid open for the world to see. There was a sense of accomplishment but a sense of trepidation that went along with it. Questions surfaced, like,

Will I be judged?

Will I be viewed differently now?

Will what I said be taken out of context?

(Although during filming it was simpler questions, like, *What will I wear?*)

I enjoyed looking at the final product and remembering what had gone on behind the scenes. It was filmed during the early part of 2021, when the pandemic-related restrictions definitely added some challenges. Then, there was the anxiety of having a section being filmed in our home. I remember the extra effort in cleaning the house, clearing the clutter, and hiding things from clear view. Since we are big-time cooks, we halted our activity to let the food smells out. And then, of course, the film team suggested, "Let's have you cook if that's what you like doing." I didn't know that the audio would make it into the final cut...and there I am complaining about the onion smell. Some *candid camera* moments!

I agreed to have my story be told because we want to break down barriers – *you don't have to be a specific type to be the science type.* My story clearly illustrates that fact. But by the same token, I also wanted to make clear the privilege and heritage I have had, of access and ambition, that is typically denied to many. I come from a family of highly educated professionals, and many have been highly accomplished in their respective fields or trailblazers in the family. Of course, I had my own share of challenges, and I talked about them. In many cases, challenges can be reframed, and they can sometimes give an individual deep motivation to grow, despite the detractors. I have seen many leaders talk about turning their challenges into an exceptional source of motivation. That sense of self-empowerment starts a positive cycle of achieving equity.

And sometimes, self-empowerment can be brought on by a behavioral shift, an identity shift. It is what I think happened to me when I was given the very visible role of Chief Science Advocate. I had to internalize this identity as a leader. I educated myself and built credibility about the topics, giving me the strength to authentically advocate for someone or something. The notion of helping those who come after me gives me context and a sense of purpose for making organizational changes, providing opportunities, and expanding strategic initiatives because that motivates me – it gives me context to lead from what I call from *my own rung of the ladder.*

It has been a privilege to be part of our science advocacy team and projects like *Not the Science Type.* I can honestly say that I didn't realize how the role would evolve and the dimensions we would delve into, but I am glad we have been able to peel back the layers of the onion on this topic and into my own experiences. I often find myself rationalizing – *if it helps someone, I should push myself to do it.* I feel it's worth it. That's what being a true advocate perhaps means. I am proud that we have brought innovation into our advocacy efforts just as we do in our products. And my family is proud of me in that I found the courage to tell my story – I am not the typical *immigrant trope*, I am not the *I always wanted to be a scientist*, I am not an *expert* in any field, I don't have an *army of people* reporting to me. I stayed authentic to my interests and stuck to my inclinations, and I survived and thrived in STEM.

I am proud that my story can give hope to others – *and that triggers my amygdala.*

———

Fear FACTOR:
Let It Go

Warming up to the hot topic of middle management...

It was during one of the coldest spells of the year that I was invited to speak at a 3M virtual Technical Manager Roundtable. Before the meeting started in earnest, the obligatory weather discussion was rendered mandatory given the fact we were in the grips of a winter freeze. Every winter, much of North America becomes a frozen tundra – sub-zero temperatures, frigid arctic air, and bone-chilling winds that accompany the phenomenon termed polar vortex. As the vortex at the poles weakens, it can no longer hold on to the cold air, and, with its grip loosening, the arctic blast seeps south and temperatures plunge through much of the continent. Most people, even hardy Minnesotans, don't venture out during this time given the dangerous lows in temperatures. Confronting fears became a topic of much discussion at the event. I think many attendees had looks of disbelief when I shared that I had already gone for my daily walk, *outdoors!*

Much of the credit goes to the pandemic times. Like many others, it forced me to spend more time outdoors and let myself be drawn into nature, not just to be out and about, but to truly appreciate it. As spring blossomed into summer, and it turned into autumn, and then ready-to-roll into winter, I had a decision to make. *Would it be like every other year, a hibernation of sorts? Or should I make a change?* A solitary, daily outdoor walk had the ability, in a very mindful and meaningful way, to break up the monotony of long days packed with virtual meetings. I had seen numerous benefits, from the boosting of mood, morale, and creativity to a sense of calm, awe, and gratitude.

As winter approached, I decided to confront the fears that have gripped me all these years. I read up on cold-induced asthma to allay my anxiety, I researched and bought winter gear (because I didn't really own any), and, I started yoga and stretching for improved balance. Let's just say the treadmill was not fired up in winter; instead, I made strides in conquering the fears that were holding me back. I took the plunge and finally overcame my fear of the Minnesota winters – I love telling that story and sharing pictures, frozen eyelashes and all.

FROZEN MIDDLE

Middle management can be one of the toughest roles in any large corporation, especially in the current heightened VUCA World. It's a time of rapid change, with accelerated advancement in science and adoption of new technologies, changing customer behaviors, and shifting market forces. The middle level of management needs to play a critical role given the increasing pressures from both upper management and employees.

The concept of "frozen middle" is believed to have been first described in 2005.[39] It essentially conveys that whatever strategies or initiatives top management decide to undertake can come to a standstill by the unwillingness and/or inability of the middle management to carry them out. In essence, every organization needs strong middle management because it is absolutely critical to its overall success. This layer of management may not have set the priorities for the organization, but they are accountable for execution, and, in many ways, for holding the various layers together. Things are further complicated and confounded with the need to lead and coordinate global teams in matrixed organizational hierarchy that recruits talent and retains knowledge while working with varying demographic groups.

ON THIN ICE

In my observations, failure to execute can not only lead to an organization, or its initiatives, being seemingly stuck, but that failure can also create a sense of confusion and chaos. The role of middle management requires balancing many elements, such as short-term focus and associated mechanics and a long-term vision with holistic wisdom, while consistently expanding the sphere of influence given a sphere of control. It is a tough job, but very rewarding if one adopts a *growth mindset*. People should opt for it for the right reasons; one must like the responsibility, be able to deal with uncertainty, and most importantly, truly enjoy working with people – *all people*. It is, of course, also the training grounds for higher pay, power, and prestigious roles within the organization.

Full disclosure: In my case, apart from a year of having direct reports, and a few years as a group leader of sorts, I have never officially been a formal people manager. For several reasons, some unfounded, it felt like a scary proposition to me when I was at the crossroads. It's always interesting to talk about what you think the role is, without ever having assumed that role in earnest. But I was asked to present my perspective, developed over the last three decades, which has incorporated ample observations, interactions, and collaborations with many technical R&D mentees and leaders in middle management. I took the roundtable dialogue as

[39] Byrnes, J., "Middle Management Excellence," *Harvard Business School Working Knowledge*, December 5, 2005.

an opportunity to walk through specific examples and highlight key attributes within the context of fostering growth and innovation in a science and technology-focused organization. Overall, it is the importance of balance, focusing on the skills, behaviors, and actions, that I think made for great managers, especially in a strong culture of employee empowerment, like at 3M.

We discussed key strategies, some that I have previously written about and those I share below, that managers can use for fostering a trusting relationship with those they manage, and really help them improve, excel, and shine. We also talked about the typical pitfalls, the icebergs to avoid – any behaviors or actions that can lead to complaints including, "My manager micromanages," or they are "always positioning and posturing," or they "only manage upwards," or they are "stuck in the job and disengaged," or they "don't have credibility with peers or upper management," to name a few. A common one that is beginning to come up more often is, "My manager doesn't recognize my contribution – my manager only promotes/supports men."

Most organizations these days have explicit goals and directives to ensure gender equity. But despite the commitment, progress remains slow toward these goals; specifically, the number of women in management roles remains low. Middle management is largely responsible for driving these strategies and making these critical advancement decisions. There has been much discussion on the role of meritocracy and the need for adequate training for middle managers, *men and women*, to understand the role of bias in their decision making – in recruitment, support, and advancement.

SNOWBALL EFFECT

Good managers educate themselves on strategic DE&I initiatives and understand their roles in driving them – they commit and lead by example, being conversant in the goals, speaking on the topic, fostering dialogue, and attending and encouraging others to attend training and DE&I events. Above all, they educate themselves, actively seek to overcome any biases and barriers, and drive equitable decisions. I have seen many managers who can effectively translate strategic priorities and provide support and guidance to the organization, while serving as an effective bridge between the layers. These are "great managers" who take risks, yet protect the people, have trust in their own capabilities, and build and foster cross-functional relationships.[40] They value candor, transparency, and open dialog, and they value diversity. They make informed decisions, they inspire – *they grow, their people grow, their influence grows.*

[40] Beck, R.J. & Harter, J., "Why Great Managers Are So Rare," *Gallup Business Journal*, n.d.

I have also seen those who struggle to recognize or break down barriers that may be getting in the middle of allowing them to fully flourish in their management role. They are fearful of change and uncomfortable in their own abilities to lead change. They may take the path of least resistance and hire people who are similar to them or similar to others in their group – it may make their job *easier* in their view and maximize the chance of group *success*. They would rather maintain *status quo* and are fearful of having to deal with people who they perceive as "different." However, this can stunt their ability to stretch their thinking and add to their experiences – they don't experience growth in their management style, and their organizations, their reputation and their output suffers.

The **FACTOR** that is typically holding many back is the fear of one or more of the following:

Failure

Anxiety & insecurity

Change acceptance

Trust issues

Organizational savvy

Relationships

If 2020 taught us anything, it is to confront our fears to live more mindful and fulfilling lives, at home and at work. It is about acceptance and making an effort to change our views, learning and developing new habits as needed to broaden our horizons, and improving things for us and those around us.

There is an immense sense of satisfaction in breaking through. I feel it when I am out in the crisp, brilliant, sun-soaked winter, and I smile through frozen eyelashes. Are there risks? Yes, but they outweigh the benefits. And it's not that the cold weather didn't affect me anymore. I figured out my it and warmed up to the idea of letting it go. That action took realization, preparation, training, and commitment to execution. It took active *management – beginning, middle, and ongoing.*

Sometimes it's important to not hold tight but let go of that fear factor. The FACTOR that holds us back. The fears that have us frozen.

— FINE PRINT —

I strongly feel that middle managers can often set the pulse of an organization. This, in my view, will remain a very critical role impacting employee morale and group outcomes. And this role has become harder yet with the sudden transition to remote work. Employees fear that their managers may not know what their contributions are, given the loss of face-to-face, everyday office interactions. Managers fear that they may not be able to maintain connectedness with all their direct reports, connections that are much needed during a complex transition. Meanwhile, they have to show empathy, create psychological safety, and inspire remote workers while the managers themselves may feel isolated with often no real support group structure, sandwiched between the hierarchy of their supervisors and their supervisees. Managers are in fact *also* at a risk of burnout and meltdowns due to exhaustion, stress, and mental fatigue.

Those who are intuitively tuned, specifically trained, or significantly experienced can make a difference by rising up to the challenge. A key aspect of this effort involves taking meaningful action, including empathetic conversations – understanding worker family situations and associated pressures, and fostering deeper relationships that encourage open communications and empower employees. It can be a truly rewarding experience for the managers to see their employees flourish through this transition. But it can be particularly stressful for those who weren't trained abundantly, or screened adequately for their managerial potential, to fulfill a role that has become even more challenging during this time. Organizations need to pay close attention to whom they groom, train, or appoint to go into these roles. The decision to go into management impacts the decision maker and those around them.

Many years ago, I was offered a management position. After much deliberation I turned it down. It was surprising to many since I did not have aspecific technical expertise – the management position would have created opportunity for me to rise up the ranks quickly. If I really am being honest, one of the reasons I turned it down is because I was too fearful – *fearful of many things that were unknowns to me at the time.* Would I be able to handle conflict, make tough decisions, share bad news? Would I be able to give honest feedback? Would my candid, direct communications create a furor? Would I be able to play the necessary office politics? Would I lose control over my family life? But above all, my biggest fear was: Would I really be able to *let it go?* Let go of things I like doing. Would I be able to delegate, work through others, resist the temptation of doing things myself? *And then, would I be able to be authentically me?*

I did all right. I did not go into management. I had my reasons at the time. And by the same token, in my role, I do delegate, I form strong relationships with others, and I know I can't do everything myself. But I know I made the right choice for me. Of course, life isn't a controlled experiment, so one will never know how that future would have played out. Oftentimes, it is not a straightforward decision, but it helps to be self-aware, and it helps to reflect. It helps to think through why one thinks they are or aren't suited for the role. And if there is fear – what is the basis for it? Can it be substantiated, validated, or minimized by talking to others in similar roles?

It's okay to get cold feet and choose, or not choose, the management path, but one needs to be okay with that decision and its consequences. It is a topic that can be revisited as situations, experiences, or understandings of the role change. What is certain is that the role of manager will change in the future given what transpired through the COVID-19 pandemic. And despite being a challenging role, in my opinion, it can also be the most impactful role – not just as training ground for the person, but for creating change and lasting impact on their organizations and the people they manage – *lighting a fire or leaving them out in the cold.*

It is also a role that is often less frequently assigned to women early on in their careers – the "broken rung" as it is called. It's the biggest obstacle keeping women from advancing in their careers – *the first step up from entry-level position to manager and its disproportionate impact on the rest of their careers.* Organizations are taking a close look at systemic practices that may be leading to this phenomenon, and I am hopeful that meaningful action will be taken to make the processes more transparent.

At the end of the day, good managers have contextual understanding of the engaged, knowledgeable leadership their role entails. They demonstrate leadership in that they can articulate a compelling vision for the work group, have the resilience to overcome adversity, and motivate employees to act and engage. Good managers know it isn't just about the products but also the *possibilities,* not just about the technology but the trends, not just about the customers but our *commitments* to the market. Above all, it's not just about the processes – it's about the *people.* People, in all their diversity, enrich an organization and fuel innovation. Those who truly understand these factors are the ones who will empower and manage to lead us through this change, fearlessly.

———

The GRANT
of an Immigrant Mindset

"What gave you strength to continue your STEM journey?"

Being featured as one of the scientists in 3M's docuseries, *Not the Science Type*, made me relive moments from my past in many ways. The experience transcended my path through a STEM education and career, as I explored memories of the mindsets I had as I navigated pivotal junctures and milestones. I must admit that while I was going through it, I never gave it much thought. But now, I find myself reflecting upon the key tenets that emerged along my journey each time I get interview questions and queries from viewers. Questions like the one above, and,

How did you deal with being the "only"?

How were you able to manage moving into completely new areas?

Why do you feel strongly about giving back?

What advice do you have for others navigating similar situations?

As is always the case, there were many factors at play, some known and some unknown to me. But I want to highlight the role of an *immigrant mindset* that has served as a backdrop to my story – and I want to emphasize being an immigrant to the United States, not in the literal sense but figuratively, as it relates to my thinking in general. There have been several articles in recent years capturing the essence of what constitutes the positive aspects of an immigrant mindset – a mindset that, among other things, prompts one to be more comfortable with discomfort, fuels the passion to create opportunity, pushes one to work harder, and gives unique perspective on a sense of purpose while paving the way.[41]

In looking back, this mindset was integral to confronting challenges and obstacles, and I hope that mentality continues to be central to the way I approach projects and initiatives. And in looking ahead there are aspects of this mindset that may be critical, post-pandemic, amidst a time of accelerated change.

---

[41] Llopis, G., "Adopt an Immigrant Mindset to Advance Your Career," *Harvard Business Review*, August 24, 2012.

IMMIGRANT MENTALITY

I had the fortune to observe elements of this mindset up-close in my parents when I was growing up. Our family had left India for England before my first birthday. It would have taken enormous courage for my parents to take this risk and commit to facing challenges head-on, and, they must have had immense confidence in their ability to overcome those challenges. While my father navigated graduate school in a foreign country, working long hours, my mother taught herself to be conversant in English and resourcefully navigated the home front. I do know this immigrant experience gave my parents a broader perspective and the ability to see things differently. Once we returned to India a few years later, it was reflected in their thinking and in our upbringing. It was also very clear that we were to work hard to make the best of any opportunity, with the recognition that stepping outside of the comfort zone, resiliently, was essential to growth and success.

In looking back, it was this mindset that perhaps also supported me when I had to move after high school from Northern India, where I grew up, to the deep South of India. Given the change of language, food, and norms, it was there that I had to confront many challenges typical of what an immigrant would face – those arising from simply not knowing the language to those resulting from cultural differences or deep-rooted biases on multiple fronts. It was especially hard for us girls from different regions who had ended up there, and we banded together to find community. We knew we would be viewed differently, and subconsciously this acceptance propelled many of us to work harder. We adapted. We learned to ignore the *noise* in the system that could potentially deter us from our path. We celebrated our differences and we supported each other.

IMMIGRANT SENTIMENTALITY

I must admit that there was also the distinct sense that I had left my hometown, my family, and friends, and I was going to have to make it count. I worked hard to navigate the new experiences and recall feeling a strange sense of satisfaction at being at the top of my engineering class. This was much to the chagrin of many of *the guys* who had certainly been less than welcoming and often judgmental regarding girls' abilities in STEM, especially what they viewed as *my kind*, seemingly confident, outgoing, and with many interests – not the typical *studious type*. As we slowly found our bearing in subsequent years, some of us also took it upon ourselves to mentor others who were in the same boat, navigating the newness. We felt it was important to us to make it easier for those who came after us.

These crucible experiences came into play when I came to the U.S. for graduate school. Although I knew the language this time, the culture, surroundings, systems, and thinking were vastly different from what I was accustomed to, and the field of study proved to be something that didn't particularly excite me. Looking back, despite switching subjects for my Ph.D. project, I can see that I subconsciously adopted the same mentality and adapted to the circumstances – the acceptance of being new and different, the commitment to seeking opportunity and learning from challenges, and the effort and strong work ethic to make a difference.

Being an immigrant from India, a collectivist society and culture, I would say there was an added sentimentality – I carried with me the realization that each person is only a small part of the greater whole. My journey lent itself to longer-term thinking, transcending above self to work with a strong purpose, make an impact, and leave a legacy. Mentorship, teaching, coaching, and building community became a part of much give-back at work and outside of work.

IMMIGRANT SENSIBILITY

It is a time of great change. Great many things need to change. *How do we change and make it great?* I do feel that in the current times, perhaps we all can adopt the essence of the immigrant mindset. This mindset has also been linked to *growth mindset.*[42] It can lead to more innovative thinking and allows one to develop the ability to seek out opportunities and be creative when confronted with lack of resources. The mindset allows one to reframe adversity and challenges as opportunities, forcing creativity while boosting resilience. In "Adopt an Immigrant Mindset to Advance Your Career,"[14] the author talks about the key ingredients of thinking like an immigrant by adopting the mindset many immigrants have – the motivation, the ability to see opportunity in challenges, and the capability to make the most of them through resilience and dogged perseverance. There is no room for *entitlement thinking,* and nothing can be taken for granted.

The immigrant mindset has also long been recognized as a key ingredient for success, and parallels have been drawn to a more entrepreneurial mindset. A study conducted in 2011 reported that more than 40% of Fortune 500 companies were founded by immigrants or their children.[43] In fact, immigrants, in comparison with native-born citizens, are more than twice as likely to start a business. There are reasons, *beyond generalizations and stereotypes,* why many immigrants are able to successfully navigate the entrepreneurial path.

I feel fortunate to have had the opportunity to inculcate this mindset and the positive attitude and attributes associated with it. I am also well aware of the aspects of privilege that have played a strong role in my journey. Among them,

[42] Pedron, Z., 2020. Why Companies Should Embed a Growing Immigrant Mindset in Their Culture. *Global,* 4, 60.
[43] Hayes II, J., "Want to Get More Done and Be More Successful? Adopt an Immigrant Mentality?" *Inc.,* December 13, 2017.

coming to U.S. on my own free will as a student in pursuit of education and the opportunity to build social capital in the process. I am also an immigrant from a country where my family was in high social standing and a history of academic orientation and educational achievement. Finally, I am part of a networked community that has done incredibly well in foreign lands. I am not delving into the role of meritocracy, immigration, and systemic issues here – I accept that there are certainly many ways to define success and firmly believe that many factors determine success.

And, there are many factors that, in fact, hinder success for many, specifically as it relates to systemic barriers, as well as diversity, equity, and inclusion challenges. There is also a significant downside to the abject romanticization of archetypal immigrant behavior – *work hard, stay under the radar, be grateful, and don't demand anything.* This can lead to marginalization and exploitation that has been central to the immigrant experience of many. It can be particularly problematic for women. As far as STEM is concerned, I have previously talked about many of the challenges that women may face, be it the constructs that are often stacked against them, the archetypes and the stereotypes, or the tokenism and typecasting that can be severely limiting – we certainly have to address these challenges. Despite singular examples, it is unfair to expect one to battle these systemic equity issues individually. However, I do feel we can draw upon the positives of an immigrant mindset. It can perhaps inspire and propel us to forge ahead and help to create a path with the set of unique gifts it brings and **GRANT** it gives:

Grit

Resourcefulness

Adaptability

Navigation skills

Transcendence

At times we all need help in building our capacity for resilience, risk-taking, and becoming grittier and more resourceful – so we can help ourselves and help others. It can help us move beyond typical leadership to a more transcendental leadership.

As we move forward in a post-pandemic world, an immigrant mindset can perhaps change our outlook and approach. You don't have to have been an immigrant to adopt the elements of the mindset, and by the same token – *given the rate of change, we all may feel like immigrants navigating new territory!* In the current times, perhaps we all can adopt the grant of the immigrant mindset.

— FINE PRINT —

In many ways, the GRANT factors have also been critical as I have navigated uncharted territory in my role as Chief Science Advocate. The role itself didn't exist at 3M, or for that matter in any other organization like ours. I have written about the feelings of self-doubt about being in this role, given that I never thought of myself as a typical science and engineering type while I was growing up. But I accepted this opportunity and feel that I subconsciously exercised the hallmark mentality, sentimentality, and sensibility in giving it the best of my ability.

It was important for me to be authentic in this role and bring in my own experiences in my STEM journey as well as what I have observed in raising my kids. I also wanted to have my own authentic voice – *do all my writing and handle my own social media*. I did not give up my *day job* as a scientist. I am currently working on a critical technology development slated to be commercialized with a product launch. I had to be very resourceful in contributing effectively to both my role as a scientist and the added responsibility in my role as a science advocate.

I must admit, I have the tendency to push myself to work harder and harder, but I did reach a point where I had to start saying "no." I needed to work in smarter ways. I also needed to say "no" more often. It was very tough, initially, to decline opportunities to speak, prominent roles in various forums, and requests for one-to-one meetings. The demands on my time grew exponentially as we started gaining visibility. I also learned how to balance the sense of gratitude on being selected for the role and assert my influence on how we shape the role, the programming, and the priorities.

I became an integral part of the process and viewed it with a growth mindset, akin to what I do in my day job – *innovating to create new products, patents, and platforms*. We collaborated to put out programming and iterated as we went along. We had to try many different things and be adaptable and flexible in our approach. Just like in our product development, real-life innovation takes imagination, experimentation, and iteration. We learned from all our experiments – *those that were successful and those that didn't perform per expectations*. And all these experiments gave us perspective and opportunity to pivot as we progressed. We gave it our all and felt proud of our efforts. As we learned, we adapted and optimized our 3M SOSI survey as well as the public launch and publicity of results.

During the pandemic we really had to be agile and flexible with our programming. It took grit and resourcefulness to navigate through these times and keep the momentum going. We adapted to the rapid change around us and were able to pull off a *pandemic pulse* survey to gain insight into this unique moment in time. We also launched 3M Science at Home with videos made do-it-yourself style within our homes – *something that I would never have expected we would do*. But these videos, which may have lacked the usual polish, added to a sense of accessibility of science as diverse scientists conducted fun and simple experiments in their own homes and recorded them.

And then of course there was *Not the Science Type*, filmed and launched during the pandemic. Producing a movie was truly a first for 3M, a new territory. And doing it during pandemic times is a remarkable achievement. And I am thankful that I have had an opportunity in this individual role as an advocate for science to take action for the collective good. The transcendence of that experience is something I don't take for granted.

———

Change, a Catalyst for Change!
CIRCLE of Reasoning

It is time to collectively shape the future of work – to shape our collective future.

I read a prediction heading into 2022 that society will change more in the next five decades than it has in the last three centuries! The COVID-19 pandemic served as an inflection point to accelerate change, and in many ways, it set off a domino effect. And suddenly, wherever you looked, change abounded. We have to be thankful to change, for the opportunity it brings. Central to that is the *future of work.* There has been a big change in the way we work, and more change is in the works as people are reassessing their relationship with work. Many have decided to quit altogether, a phenomenon dubbed as the "The Great Resignation." Others are up for the "The Great Reshuffle" – they look to change and are willing to reskill in order to find compatibility with the way they want to work. In addition, there is a need for "The Great Reset," *why* they want to work and for *whom* they want to work. Overall, there is a desire to create a work experience that is more equitable and inclusive and, at the end of the day, feels more fulfilling.

INNER CIRCLE

I was invited to give the opening keynote for the 2021 National Convention of SASE – Society for Asian Scientists and Engineers. The virtual SASE Professional Conference focused on how to "Unlock the Leadership Potential of Asian Professionals." SASE research shows that people with Asian heritage are nearly 50% less likely to be promoted into middle management and executive positions as their counterparts with European heritage. SASE refers to this as the "Asian Leadership Gap" – which creates a tremendous amount of untapped potential for companies. The lack of Asian leadership representation has also been dubbed the "bamboo ceiling," analogous to the glass ceiling that women hit.[44] The conference tracks were focused on professional development opportunities, based on research findings, regarding how Asian American leaders can find, inculcate, and leverage their superpowers to lead, advance, and succeed.

Having served as chair for the 3M Asian Affinity Group – A3CTION – and in

---

[44] Hyun, J., 2005. *Breaking the Bamboo Ceiling: Career Strategies for Asians,* HarperCollins.

my role on the Advisory Board, we have poured over research on the topic of Asian heritage leadership over the years. Much of the professional development discussion centers around developing communication and influencing skills, building organizational savvy, navigating hierarchy, and bolstering an innovative mindset for a healthy relationship with risk. These, of course, are attributes that everyone should be working on for professional development, regardless of race, ethnicity, or gender. But they are often highlighted as areas of improvement for Asian heritage professionals in STEM careers. Asians and Asian Americans can often feel invisible, underappreciated, and taken for granted.

CIRCLE OF INFLUENCE

We all know what else has been invisible, underappreciated, and taken for granted – *science!* 3M SOSI results have clearly shown us that. In fact, that is the reason why my role was created in 2018 – *we needed to advocate for science*. But since the pandemic, as I have talked about the results of 3M SOSI 2020 and 2021, we learned that science was having its moment – *skepticism had gone down and trust was higher*. Science and scientists led the way and led us out of the pandemic with the gift of science in the vaccine. In the public's perception, when the need arose, science stepped up and science delivered. That is why science got noticed.

But we know science was always delivering – *it just wasn't recognized for doing so*. The pandemic brought it to the forefront and, suddenly, it was not just viewed as important, but instilled hope for the future, as seen in the 2021 results. As I have discussed previously, there are perhaps many reasons behind the change in perception – with our health involved, science got personal. Scientists also attempted to build a trusting relationship with society. There was the criticality of social sciences and humanities that featured prominently in the story of science through the pandemic, and it resonated with the public. In many ways it wasn't the output of science per se, but it was also about the contextual backdrop that allowed science to emerge from the shadows and grow its influence. Just as it did for science, the change around us offers a very unique opportunity – *to become visible and make influence grow*.

FULL CIRCLE

Change of such magnitude spotlights opportunity. The social effects of the COVID-19 pandemic brought opportunity for more collectivism in our thinking, more introspection and integration with the externalities, respect for the past and responsibility for the future, and the urgent need for ecological balance and harmony in our relationship with the environment. What also became very clear:

there wasn't some linear model that could be studied, but in fact these issues were very much *circular, interdependent, intertwined.*

Gaps have been exposed in the current structures, systems, and models. As people move on from the immediate impacts of the pandemic, we want to learn from the past and move forward with purpose. The importance of humanities and social sciences and the sense of unity and connectivity is paramount. This is the message I took to the conference and the message that resonated with my audience – *these are the classical tenets of Asian philosophy, hallmarks of Eastern cultures, and in fact, deep-rooted values in African and Indigenous cultures as well.* The deep sense of community, the integration of deference for the elderly, and the immense focus on children's future are cultural elements imbibed right from childhood. Asian immigrants and children of immigrants often see these elements woven through their upbringing, and these often become fabric of their being.

Asian scientists and STEM professionals have the added experience of further mastering linear thinking and analytical cognition, which are often critical in scientific training. But research has shown that the thinking process for most Asians, at its core, is more dialectical[45] – the kind of thinking that takes into account the rich context and the inherent contradictions. It is the kind of thinking that accommodates the circularity of time and constant non-linear aspect of change, and it strives for the compromises needed. The COVID-19 pandemic highlighted the need to bring together the diversity of both dialectical and linear thinking, as well as holistic and analytic cognition. Asian heritage STEM professionals have a lot to offer in cracking the code of where we need to get to. As the reset happens, and leaders and organizations seek to develop a strategy, it is time to step up, get a seat at the table, and help drive much needed change –justifiably so.

WINNER'S CIRCLE

We need to bring in hallmark dialectical thinking of Eastern cultures into our organizational mindset. There is no right or wrong here; this is not East or West, linear or circular, analytic or holistic – *it's time for true diversity of thought.* It's time to bring in elements of collectivist thinking that emphasize community, collaboration, harmony, and balance, together with individual responsibility of voicing one's own opinion and self-expression. It's not a zero-sum game – we will all win if we can institute changes to bring this diverse thinking into our workplace. Above all, you don't have to be Asian or Asian American to benefit from this Asian leadership

---

45 de Oliveira, S. & Nisbett, R.E., 2017. Culture Changes How We Think About Thinking: From "Human Interference" to "Geography of Thought," *Perspectives on Psychological Science, 12*(5), 782-790.

edge. It just takes integration of these elements, which seem to be much needed for the "future of work."

I also emphasized that just because you have Asian heritage doesn't mean you will practice it. It will take conscious effort – *just being Asian isn't enough!* One has to take initiative – that's the change we have to make. It requires individuals to step up, build relationships, and communicate. If it seems hard, and it is uncharacteristic, we need to remind ourselves we are not doing it for us as individuals – *we are doing it for community.* That reframing is critical to get over the internal cultural barriers and step into change. *All diversity is good diversity.*

I invited everyone to take initiative in their workplace and consider themselves key assets in helping their organization. It's not just about the day-to-day tasks or technical competence. It's also about becoming a stronger voice in the strategies and the tactics, the planning, and the execution. It's about bringing a unique perspective with dialectical thinking to help outline the contradictions, the connectedness, the complexity, and the circularity of issues at hand, to lead the compromise needed to move forward with a holistic mindset. Full **CIRCLE** with:

Collectivism and context

Inner journey and integration

Respect and responsibility

Culture and community

Long-term context and cognition

Environmental harmony and balance

I appreciated the opportunity to partner with SASE and applaud their dedication to the advancement of Asian heritage scientists and engineers so they can achieve their full career potential. It is indeed time to unlock that potential by locking in a commitment to change.

We can be thankful for this time of great change – the impetus for all of us to become more self-aware, more accessible, take more initiative, and become more impactful. The current time of change is the best time to change so we can authentically own our space – *in future and the present, at work, and in our lives.*

— FINE PRINT —

I had to wrestle through some inner conflict as I prepared my keynote for SASE. The process brought back many of the reservations I have had on how simplistically regions on the map are often clubbed together and given an identity or a label. I recall when I first started as the Chair of A3CTION, our 3M Asian heritage network, it took effort to get past the idea of Asians as a homogenous and monolithic group, especially given all the diversity in the diaspora.

However, as I interacted with the advisory board and the steering committee to lead A3CTION, it became evident that, despite the obvious differences, there were many aspects that connected us together – *specifically as it relates to professional challenges and cultural stereotypes.* Above all, the umbrella was a way to find community in these somewhat loosely tied networks.

In this role, I learned a lot – it truly enriched my professional experience and enhanced my leadership skills. We had great discussions regarding the challenges faced by Asians and Asian Americans. Among them were factors such as social and communication skills, as well as cultural and mindset paradigms, that may oftentimes be at odds with what is valued in Western corporate, and even pop-culture, expectations of leadership, including the personality of said leaders. Then, of course, there is the prevalent *model minority* myth and the pervasive stereotype of *techie Asians* – technically sound workers with limited management savvy or missing skills that are typical of the mainstream go-getters. And often, as is the case with women, stepping out of the stereotypical behavior can lead to being penalized. The fact that many of us have immigrant identities further adds to the challenge – an identity that often brings the tendency to just be grateful, work hard, and lay low. Living up to this so-called model behavior stereotype can in fact serve to limit Asians and drive a racial divide with other communities of color. But with the recent racial unrest, and related awakening, it has been heartwarming to see the high levels of solidarity.

Given the COVID-19 pandemic, and that folks may be reeling from the aftermath – dealing with the changes and feeling the uncertainty – it made me wonder if I should craft my message differently in this time of change. A change in the messaging – change from what we often hear in terms of *gaps.* I have previously talked about my views on what is called the "confidence gap" for women and how to reframe it as an *edge.* It is 2021, I thought. I could not imagine talking about gaps or about faking it. I felt the need to turn the page: *Isn't all the change around us a catalyst to change how we get to define the next normal?* Or rather, what should be normal, next? Isn't it time to truly capitalize on bringing your whole self to work for the future of work?

And that is why I decided not to resign myself to the same advice, the same old messaging. Instead, I reshuffled the deck and reset the vision with focus on the aspects of dialectical thinking that could be an asset to any leader, any organization. With all the change around us, it is a great time to refresh the dated playbooks, the old styles of what constitutes leadership, and the stereotypical image of a leader. Individual voices need to be heard for the sake of collective good. It is often easy to dismiss the need for dialectical thinking given the desire to move fast. But this so-called fast pace leaves behind many and will delay progress eventually. In my view, it is a great time for dialectical thinkers to step up and help their organizations with realistic goal-setting and holistic decision-making. It is time to be on the radar – and lift your organizations to off-the-chart heights. It is all about balance – *yin and yang*.

It is time for *karma* – good actions and intentions to influence our good work for our collective good.

_____

"I'm convinced of this: Good done anywhere is good done everywhere...
As long as you're breathing, it's never too late to do some good."

– Dr. Maya Angelou,
American poet, writer, and civil rights activist

ACKNOWLEDGMENTS

To my parents for their blessings, my friends and extended family for their good wishes, my husband Raghu for his love, support, and encouragement, and my adult children Aadarsh and Manashree for the inspiration they provide.

Thanks to everyone at 3M, including Robert Brittain and the extended SOSI team. Thanks also to SWE, the team at the David James Group, and my editor Eli Trybula for helping me understand my fine print as I put in words what is at the heart of the transitions, reflections, and actions from the last two years.

BIBLIOGRAPHY

3M, September 14, 2020. *3M to invest 50 million over 5 years to address racial opportunity gaps* [Press release]. https://news.3m.com/3M-to-invest-50-million-over-5-years-to-address-racial-opportunity-gaps.

3M, "Science at Home," https://www.3m.com/3M/en_US/gives-us/education/science-at-home/. Accessed January 24, 2022.

Appel, M. & Kronberger, N., 2012. Stereotypes and the Achievement Gap: Stereotype Threat Prior to Test Taking, *Educational Psychology Review*, 24(4), 609-635.

Baratta, M., "Pandemic 'Logic': What we tell ourselves to survive," *Psychology Today*, October 15, 2021.

Beck, R.J. & Harter, J., "Why Great Managers Are So Rare," *Gallup Business Journal*, n.d.

Beghetto, R.A. & Kaufman, J.C., 2007. Toward a Broader Conception of Creativity: A Case for "mini-c" Creativity, *Psychology of Aesthetics, Creativity, and the Arts*, 1(2), 73.

Braw, E., "What the *Ever Given* Taught the World," Foreign Policy, November 10, 2021.

Byrnes, J., "Middle Management Excellence," *Harvard Business School Working Knowledge*, December 5, 2005.

Cyr, E.N. et al., 2021. Mapping social exclusion in STEM to men's implicit bias and women's career costs, *PNAS*, 118, 40.

D'Agostino, "'We Are the World': Inside Pop Music's Most Famous All-Nighter," *Esquire*, June 24, 2020.

de Oliveira, S. & Nisbett, R.E., 2017. Culture Changes How We Think About Thinking: From "Human Interference" to "Geography of Thought," *Perspectives on Psychological Science*, 12(5), 782-790.

Deshpandé, R., Mintz, O., & Currim, I.S., "3 tactics to overcome COVID-19 vaccine hesitancy," *World Economic Forum*, June 28, 2021.

Diekman, A.B. & Steinberg, M., 2013. Navigating Social Roles in Pursuit of Important Goals: A Communal Goal Congruity Account of STEM Pursuits. *Social and Personality Psychology Compass*, 7(7), 487-501.

Ertl, B., Luttenberger, S., & Paechter, M., 2017. The Impact of Gender Stereotypes on the Self-Concept of Female Students in STEM Subjects with an Under-Representation of Females, *Frontiers in Psychology*, 8, 703.

Estrada et al., 2016. Improving Underrepresented Minority Student Persistence in STEM, *CBE – Life Sciences Education*, 15(3), es5.

Fetterman, A.K. & Robinson, M.D., 2014. What Can Metaphors Tell Us about Personality? *In Mind: the inquisitive mind, social psychology for you*, 20.

Gallagher, M.W. & Lopez, S.J., 2018. *The Oxford Handbook of Hope*, Oxford University Press.

Gaucher, D., Friesen, J., & Kay, A.C., 2011. Evidence That Gendered Wording in Job Advertisements Exists and Sustains Gender Inequality, *Journal of Personality and Social Psychology*, *101*(1), 109.

Gino, F. & Coffman, K., "Unconscious Bias Training That Works," *Harvard Business Review*, September - October 2021.

Gorman, A., *Call Us What We Carry: Poems*, Viking Books, December 2021.

Grant, A., "There's a Name for the Blah You're Feeling: It's Called Languishing," *The New York Times*, April 19, 2021.

Hayes II, J., "Want to Get More Done and Be More Successful? Adopt an Immigrant Mentality?" *Inc.*, December 13, 2017.

Hyun, J., 2005. *Breaking the Bamboo Ceiling: Career Strategies for Asians*, HarperCollins.

Kapoor, H. & Kaufman, J.C., 2020. Meaning-Making Through Creativity During COVID-19, *Frontiers in Psychology*, 11, 3659.

Kaufman, J.C. & Beghetto, R.A., 2009. Beyond Big and Little: The Four C Model of Creativity, *Review of General Psychology*, *13*(1), 1-12.

Kowalski, K., A Simple Wellness Strategy: MEDS (Meditation, Exercise, Diet, Sleep), SLOWW.co/meds, February 2019.

Lee, D.N., "A Dream Deferred: How access to STEM is denied to many students before they get in the door good," *Scientific American*, January 24, 2013.

Llopis, G., "Adopt an Immigrant Mindset to Advance Your Career," *Harvard Business Review*, August 24, 2012.

Makarova, E., Aeschlimann, B., & Herzog, W., 2019. The Gender Gap in STEM Fields: The Impact of the Gender Stereotype of Math and Science on Secondary Students' Career Aspirations, *Frontiers in Education*, 4, 60.

McGuire et al., 2020. Beating the virus: an examination of the crisis communication approach taken by New Zealand Prime Minister Jacinda Ardern during the Covid-19 pandemic, *Human Resource Development International*, 23(4), 361-379.

Muis, K.R., et al., 2021. Epistemic Emotions and Epistemic Cognition Predict Critical Thinking About Socio-Scientific Issues, *Frontiers in Education*, 6, 121.

National Academy of Engineering, 2008. Changing the Conversation: *Messages for Improving Public Understanding of Engineering*. The National Academies Press.

Newman, T., "Science elicits hope in Americans – its positive brand doesn't need to be partisan," *The Conversation*, July 23, 2020.

The Nobel Prize in Physiology or Medicine 2017 awarded to Jeffrey C. Hall, Michael Roshbash, and Michael W. Young.

Pedron, Z., 2020. Why Companies Should Embed a Growing Immigrant Mindset in Their Culture? *Global*, 4, 60.

Petriglieri, G., "The Psychology Behind Effective Crisis Leadership," *Harvard Business Review*, April 22, 2020.

Science Counts, 2018. "How Americans View Science in Society: A Scientific Approach to a Difficult Problem," Accessed January 24, 2022.

Seth, J., 2008. *Namaste! Namaste!...and other Hindi songs based on popular nursery rhymes*, self-published, Blurb.

Simmons, R., "Why Failure Hits Girls So Hard," *Time*, August 25, 2015.

Tang et al., 2021. Creativity as a Means to Well-Being in Times of COVID-19 Pandemic: Results of a Cross-Cultural Study, *Frontiers in Psychology*, 12, 265.

Urbina-Blanco et al., 2020. A Diverse View of Science to Catalyse Change, *Journal of the American Chemical Society*, 14(34), 14393-14396.

Wheatley, M.J., "It's An Interconnected World," *Shambhala Sun*, April 2002.

Yong, E., "What We Learn From 50 Years of Kids Drawing Scientists," *The Atlantic*, March 20, 2018.

"'You Guys': Is There A Better Option?" *Dictionary.com*, December 19, 2018.

ABOUT THE AUTHOR

Jayshree Seth, Ph.D., is a Corporate Scientist at 3M Company, headquartered in St. Paul, Minnesota, USA, where she has worked for over 28 years. She holds 72 patents on a variety of innovations, with several others pending. She currently leads applied technology development for sustainable industrial products in 3M's Industrial Adhesives and Tapes Division. She is also 3M's first-ever Chief Science Advocate and is charged with communicating the importance of science in everyday life, breaking down barriers, and building excitement around STEM careers. She is very passionate about teaching, coaching, and mentoring. A globally sought-after speaker on a multitude of topics such as innovation, leadership, and science advocacy, Dr. Seth has been interviewed in national and international media, and she has been featured in 3M brand campaigns and commercials.

Dr. Seth joined 3M in 1993 after earning an M.S. and Ph.D. in Chemical Engineering from Clarkson University in New York. A Distinguished Alumni Award recipient from her alma mater, REC Trichy India, now NIIT Trichy, she earned a B. Tech. in Chemical Engineering. Dr. Seth is the fourth woman and first woman engineer to attain the highest technical designation of Corporate Scientist at 3M, as well as induction into the 3M Carlton Society, which honors the very best among the scientific community. She is also a certified Design for Six Sigma Black Belt.

At 3M, she has served on the CEO Inclusion Council, chaired the Asian and Asian American Employee Network (A3CTION), and serves on its Advisory Board, as well as serving on the steering team for 3M Women's Leadership Forum Technical (WLF-T) chapter. She also serves on the Board of the Science Museum of Minnesota, Engineering Advisory Council for Clarkson University, AAAS Committee on Science, Engineering and Public Policy (COSEPP), and the Advisory Group of Aspen Institute Our Future Is Science (OFIS) program. She has received numerous 3M excellence awards and a record-setting number of intrapreneurial grants to drive innovation. She was conferred the 2020 Achievement Award from the Society of Women Engineers (SWE), the 2019 International Women & Technologies' Le Tecnovisionarie® award for sustainability, and the 2020 Woman of Distinction by Girl Scouts River Valley, and was also among engineers selected to attend the National Academy of Engineering's (NAE) 14th annual U.S. Frontiers of Engineering symposium. Jayshree was also the first-ever winner of a Gold Stevie® Award in the new "Female Thought Leaders of the Year" category in the 18th annual

Festival and was featured in Brand Storytelling 2022 a sanctioned event at Sundance Film Festival. She is the author of *The Heart of Science:Engineering Footprints, Fingerprints, & Imprints.*

Dr. Seth grew up in India in a university town in the foothills of the Himalayas and at the banks of the River Ganges canal. She has over 15 journal publications based on her graduate work, co-authoring several with her husband, who also works at 3M. They enjoy extending science, creativity, and innovation into their kitchen. They have two adult children. Dr. Seth enjoys experiencing other cultures and she is also an avid reader, writer, and poet.

Dr. Seth is active on social media. You can follow her on LinkedIn, Twitter, and Instagram. Twitter: @jseth2, Insta: sethjayshree

If you loved
The Heart of Science: Engineering Fine Print,
we think you'll enjoy:

The Heart of Science Book One:
Engineering Footprints, Fingerprints, & Imprints

Explore big ideas with the Science Advocate in Chief through this collection of insights, reflections, and tips. Compiled from a successful corporate career that spans over 25 years, 70 patents, and national and international accolades, Dr. Jayshree Seth discusses our relationship with science and engineering while offering her unique perspective on topics surrounding advocacy, interdisciplinary contexts, thoughtful leadership, and inclusive progress. Told with her story as a backdrop, including her childhood experiences and those of her children, Jayshree shares what she's learned in this memorable and entertaining compilation. The Heart of Science is for anyone involved or interested in Science, Technology, Engineering, and Math (STEM) fields, including students, parents, and professionals. Jayshree Seth, Ph.D., is a corporate scientist and chief science advocate for 3M Company, where she has worked for over 27 years to advance science and develop new technologies and environmentally sustainable industrial products. Dr. Seth currently holds 70 patents on a variety of innovations, with several pending. She was the fourth woman and first female engineer inducted into the prestigious 3M Carlton Society. In 2020, Jayshree was awarded the Society for Women Engineers (SWE) highest 'Achievement Award'. Speaking to national and international audiences, her professional roles have taken her to 15 countries to collaborate on projects and address topics of innovation, leadership, science communication and student engagement, advocating for diversity in Science, Technology, Engineering, and Mathematics (STEM). All proceeds of this book go to the Jayshree Seth Scholarship for Women of Color in STEM to be administered by the Society of Women Engineers. The scholarship is aimed at helping underrepresented minorities advance in STEM education and professions related to engineering and technology.

Made in the USA
Monee, IL
12 November 2022

17636255R00077